Basic Religious books of THE HINDUS

Basic Religious books of THE HINDUS

Manju Sehgal

PRABHAT
PRAKASHAN

Published by
PRABHAT PRAKASHAN PVT. LTD.
4/19 Asaf Ali Road,
New Delhi-110 002 (INDIA)
e-mail: prabhatbooks@gmail.com

ISBN 978-93-5322-438-7
BASIC RELIGIOUS BOOKS OF THE HINDUS
by Smt. Manju Sehgal

Edition
2025

Price
₹ 400.00 (Rupees Four Hundred only)

Printed at
R-Tech Offset Printers, Delhi

Dr. Karan Singh

वेदाहमेतं पुरुषम्महान्तं आदित्यवर्णम्

3, Nyaya Marg
Chanakyapuri
New Delhi-110 021
Tel: (011) 2611-5291
2611-1744
Fax: (91-11) 2687-3171
2462-7102

Foreword

Hindustan has an extraordinary an unique wealth of scriputres, not only because they go far back at least 5000 years in time, but also because of the sheer size of the scriptural corpus. It is amazing that most of this has come down for centuries through sheer memory, and was only reduced to writing in the last couple of centuries. So large and rich are the foundational books of Hinduism that people are often bewildered by its sheer immensity and diversity, It is, therefore, useful to have a single volume introduction to help in identify in those texts that form the foundation of our civilizational heritage: We live in time so great stress and conflict, when old structures are breaking and new ones are still struggling to be born. At such a juncture we look into our scriptures, not in order to go back in time but to seek inspiration and a sense of direction in our lives.

Our religious texts fall into two main divisions: Shruti which consists of direct utterances of inspired rishis. These include the Vedas, the Brahmanas, the Aranyakas and, above all, the Upanishads. The Upanishads are in fat the master texts of Hinduism, and contain a wealth of knowledge and inspiration which in fact becomes increasingly relevant as we move forward into the nuclear age. The concept of the all pervasive divine: the Brahman, and the spark of that divinity in each human being; the Atman, are the key concepts of the Upanishads, and joining them is the ultimate goal of human existence. There are multiple paths to this unity, which collectively are called Yogas, which means to join. These include Gyana Yoga, the Way of Wisdom; Bhakti Yoga, and Way of Devotion Karma Yoga, the Way of Dedicated Works, and Raja Yoga the Royal Path of the breath and inner consciousness. The Upanishads, specially the 11 major ones, give us the foundational beliefs and practices of what is now known as Vedanta.

The second category is known as Smriti. Whereas Shruti is something that is heard, the Smriti is something that is remembered, and all the other scriptures, including the Puranas, the Mahabharata, the Ramayana and numerous other texts fall into this category. Even the great Bhagwatgita, although of crucial significance, is a derivative text, based essentially on the Upanishads. There is a famous shloka that likens the Upanishad to the cows, Shri Krishana to the cowherd, Arjuna to the calf who, alongwith other wise people, drink the divine milk of the Gita.

It is good that recently for the first time a 12 volume Encyclopaedia of Hinduism has been published which covers in great detail all aspects of our scriptures as well as the Buddhist and Jain contributions. I have written a long Foreword to the Encyclopaedia which is taken from my book **Essays on Hinduism** (Ratna Sagar). Manju Sehgal has rendered useful service by presenting the major religious texts of Hinduism for the general reader. I am sure this will be useful for the those who are interested in our rich and inclusive cultural heritage.

(Karan Singh)

Preface

The growing complexity of life has changed the simple life pattern of early home life. Mythology is an integral part of religion. It is necessary for any great culture to rest on stable spiritual foundation and function as a life giving inspiration and guidance. There are still few who know about the literature written by Ved Vyas, Valmiki or Tulsidas. I believe today everyone is so busy in their lives that they do not have the time to read the religious books like Vedas, Puranas, Upanishads, Smirits, Mahabharata, Bhagvad Gita and Ram Charita Manas. In fact, it is also a difficult task to collect these books and read them. For the last few years, I have been contemplating writing a book of such kind which would reflect Indian culture, religion, literature, induce people to do good *karmas* and to look forward in life. With God as my guide and the religious sentiments of my parents, I have been inspired to write this book *Basic Religious Books of the Hindus*. My father late Shri Kishan Kumar Mehrotra devoted his whole life for the service of others and giving love to everyone who came in his contact. He felt sad and happy after seeing the miseries and happiness of others. He was a complete spiritual personality and had complete faith in God. When he used to sit in meditation, people made use of his presence. His main aim of life was to do good to others, love them and help them. There was no desire left till the end of his life. Such person, we hardly see around us anymore. My father inherited all that from his father late Shri Ram Prasad Mehrotra, whose life was completely merged with Ramayana. He knew verbally all the couplets of Ramayana and when he used to sing them lying on his bed which was on the street side, people who were passing by used to stand and listen to him. My grandmother was also a simple, religious lady and helping others was the aim of her life. My mother late Smt. Mohini Mehrotra was a devoted wife who believed in rituals, helping the poor, especially the brahmins and had complete faith in God. This book is an attempt to give the gist of the main religious books of the Hindus so that the reader can read it easily, understand it and adopt the learnings in their lives.

Vedas prescribe some regulations and if someone follows it, one will be free from material entanglement. Rig Veda contains *suktas* and hymns in praise of gods like Indra, Varuna, Surya, Asvins, Usas, Ratri, Vayu, Jal, Brahaspati, Prithvi, Agni, Soma, Prajapati, Brahma, Aditya, etc. Yajurveda inspires human beings to do good *karma* and gives knowledge of the sacrificial formulas for liturgy. Samveda gives knowledge of the melodies for chanting. The hymns contained in this are more lyrical in nature and suggest to the early musical traditions of the Vedic people. Arthava Veda gives knowledge of the magic formulas, charms and the herbs for recovering diseases, ill effects, political affairs, marriage, funerals, etc. Puranas are the post-vedic texts which contain a complete narrative of the history of Universe from creation to destruction. There are eighteen Puranas, each named after a deity Brahma, Vishnu and Shiva.

The Upanishads represent the essence of the Vedas. The basic teaching of it is that the essence of all beings and things is the divine spirit called the Brahman. The

Smritis written to explain and elaborate the Vedas, making them understandable and more meaningful to the general population. Bhagvad Gita is in a form of a dialogue between Arjuna and Lord Krishna, his charioteer. Arjuna wants to withdraw from the battle but Krishna teaches him that he (Arjuna) must do his duty and he argues that death does not destroy the soul and that knowledge, work and devotion are all paths to salvation and that the central value in life is that of loyalty to God.

Mahabharata is not only an epic but it also tells the tale of heroic people, containing a code of life, a philosophy of social and ethical relations. Ram Charita Manas is a story of a king and his four sons. It provides the guidelines for an ideal family life (*Parivarik Jeevan*), an ideal king (*Raj Dharma*) and an ideal mother (*Matri Dharma*). It also talks about devotion (*Bhakti*), knowledge (*Gyan*), renunciation (*Varigya*) and good behaviour (*Sadachar*).

Before writing this book, first of all, I bow to Ganpati to whom I believe, help me in finishing this book. Then I bow to Brahma who is the originator, preserver and destroyer. Then I put the photograph of Lord Krishna before my eyes, who killed Kans and Jarasan, did many acts that people hear and read about, have faith in Him and attain the Supreme Power.

I am also grateful to Mr. Anant Misra who is like my son and who introduced me to Ms. Pranamika who did the job of typing of the script with utmost devotion and sincerity. She took out time from her busy schedule to complete this book and I wish her all the best in life.

Special thanks to late Shri Bal Kumar Khare who always insisted me to write this book. I am sure he will be showering his blessings on me from heavenly abode.

I am thankful to my daughter Neha for helping me in carrying out the editing work. God bless you my dear.

I am really grateful to my elder sister Smt. Sheela Tandon, who retired as Vice-Principal of the Central School of Bareilly. Without her co-operation and guidance, I won't be able to complete my book. She took keen interest in the compilation and showed me the right direction. Due to her tireless devotion and selfless commitment, the book has weathered every obstacle that has come in its way.

Last but not least, I would like to express that if you, your family, friends find this book useful for a better understanding of the religious books; if it enhances your religion, I would find my efforts worthwhile. I hope and pray that you will treasure this unique book as a useful reference to Hindu religion and philosophy.

Contents

VEDAS

1
Vedas

The word "Veda" is derived from the root word "vid". It means to know or knowledge. The Vedas are considered to be sacred and described as '*apaurushiya*' which means not man made or not written by man. It is not known for sure how the hymns have come into existence or who were the earliest recipients of this divine knowledge. It is believed by Vedic tradition that Vedas exist eternally and God brings them out at the beginning of each cycle of creation for the benefit of the worlds. The Vedas are considered to be the source books of religious knowledge. The seven ancient rishis, called Saptrishis, were the earliest recipients of this knowledge. Since Vedic hymns were only heard, they constitute the Shruti literature of Hindu tradition.

The Vedic hymns that we know are but an insignificant part of a vast body of knowledge that resides in the higher realms and are known only to a chosen few. The Vedas are meant to protect '*dharma*' and maintain cosmic order. They serve as a connecting link between the gods of the higher realms and humans as they are common to both. The Vedas are not mere magical chants to appease gods or seek their blessings but cryptic prayers in which are hidden many mysteries and symbols. They do produce magical results in the physical worlds, although that is not the only reason why they have been revealed to us.

Vedic tradition has been preserved for several centuries through a strict system of memorization. Students would memorize the hymns day after day and year after year under the close supervision of a teacher till they remembered each and every word and its pronunciation by heart. No derivations and exceptions were allowed as the hymns were divine in origin and the human being had no authority to change them or amend them even by mistake. The Vedic hymns were used in *Karma Kanda* and performing the rituals. For a very long time, the Vedas became mere books of chants and rituals while their study and recitation became the exclusive privilege of a few priestly families; except for the aranyakas and the upnishads which were studied exclusively in small groups by people dwelling in the forests and herimtages.

The Vedas are divided in three parts:

1. The Samhitas
2. The Brahmanas
3. The Upanishads, the Aranyakas and the Sutra literature

The Samhitas

The Samhitas are the main textual portions of the Vedas containing the hymns or *Suktas*.

The Brahmanas

These are commentaries in prose on the hymns of the Vedas. They serve as guides for the Brahman priests to understand the purpose of the *Samhitas*. They explain the meaning of the hymns and the procedures to be followed while performing various sacrifices.

The Upanishads

The Upanishads constitute the end part of the Vedas (*Vedanta*). They deal with philosophical and mystical aspects of the Vedas.

The Aranyakas

These are the forest books and are the concluding portion of the Vedas. They are about the philosophical aspect of the Vedas and are meant for the people leading ascetic lives in the middle of the forests.

There are mainly four Vedas in Vedic literature:

1. Rigveda – Rigveda contains *suktas* or hymns.
2. Samveda – it is known as the book of chants.
3. Yagurveda – Yagurveda is known as the book of the *Yajus* (sacrificial prayers).
4. Atharveda – this *Samhita* contains mostly magical chants which alludes to the growing influence of the native kings over the Aryan traditions.

The Vedas constitute the base as well as the hub of the Hindu tradition. For centuries, they served as the source books of standards (*Pramana*) to test the validity of philosophical statements. If truth was not supported by Vedas, it was not accepted as a philosophical truth. Those who disregarded this principle were considered as heretics and outside the fold of Hinduism. Even today many scholars tend to define a person a Hindu only if he or she accepts the authority of Vedas. The mystery of human welfare lies only in the Vedas.

Rigveda

Rigveda Samhita contains 1028 *Suktas* or hymns, divided into ten divisions or *mandalas*. There are 10,552 *mantras* in the 1028 *suktas* which are very inspiring. The main aim of these *mantras* is to purify the thoughts of man. Each *mandala* corresponds with the name of a rishi who was probably instrumental in its creation.

The Rigveda is undoubtedly the oldest literary monument of the Indo-European languages. The religion of the Rigveda is concerned with the worship of gods that are largely personifications of the powers of nature. The hymns are mainly invocations of these gods and are meant to accompany the oblation of Soma juice and the fire sacrifice of melted butter. The gods are usually stated in the Rigveda to be thirty in number. The gods were conceived as human in appearance. The arms of the Sun are nothing more than his rays and the tongue and the limbs of Agni merely denote his flames.

Some of the gods appear equipped as warriors, especially Indra, others are described as priests, especially Agni and Brahaspati. The favourite food of men is also that of gods consisting of milk, butter, grain, etc. Their favourite drink is the exhilarating juice of the Soma plant. The home of the gods is heaven, the third heaven or the highest step of Vishnu, where cheered by draughts of Soma they live a life of bliss.

Gods are constantly described as great, mighty and powerful. They regulate the order of nature and vanquish the potent powers of evil. They hold sway over all creatures. The fulfilment of desires is dependent on them. They are benevolent beings who bestow prosperity on mankind.

The Vedic gods may most conveniently be classified as deities of heaven, air and earth. The celestial gods are Dyaus, Varuna, Mitra, Surya, Savitr, Pusan and Asvins; and the goddesses are Usas, Dawn and Ratri. The atmospheric gods are Indra, Apamnapat, Rudra, the Maruts, Vayu, Parjanyu and the Waters. The terrestrial deities are Prithvi, Agni and the Soma and some rivers that are personified and invoked in Rigveda. The most important is Prajapati 'Lord of creatures'.

Literary Merit of Rigveda

The diction of the hymns is on the whole natural and simple considering their great antiquity, the hymns are composed with a remarkable degree of metrical skill and command of language. Rigveda contains much genuine poetry. As the gods are mostly connected with natural phenomena, the praises addressed to them give rise to much beautiful and noble imagery. The degree of literary merit in different hymns naturally varies a good deal but the average is remarkably high.

By Vedic gods, we mean those divinities who are mentioned in the four Vedas. The principal Vedic gods are said to be 33 in number, namely eight Vasus, eleven Rudras, twelve Adityas, Indra and Prajapati Brahma.

Indra

Indra is most popular and powerful of the Vedic deities. He is the Lord of heavens and is invoked alone in about one-fourth of the hymns of the Rigveda. He is the favourite national God of the Vedic people. He is primarily a God of thunderstorm who vanquishes the demons of drought or darkness. He is also the God of battle who aids the victorious Aryan in overcoming his aboriginal foes.

He rides a white elephant called "Airavata" and wields the dazzling weapon of lightening called Vajrayudh made by another God Tvastur. He fought many battles to drive the demons away and ensure the victory of gods. He also destroyed many cities of enemies. He slayed Vratasura and killed the demon of the dark skies with his weapon and released the cows that were held in captivity by him.

According to Kena Upanishad, he is the only God to have gone nearest to Brahmanand and was to know him as Brahman. This act of him earned him the right to become the ruler of heavens. According to Chandogya Upanishad, he studies under Prajapati Brahma and learned the secrets of immortality. In the images, Indra is generally shown with four arms and riding on a white elephant. Sometimes he is described as armed with bow and arrows; he also carries a hook (*ankusa*).

As Indra is more addicted to Soma than any of the other gods, the common epithet 'Soma-drinks' is characteristic of him. This beverage stimulates him to carry out his warlike deeds. For the slaughter of Vrtra, he is said to have drunk three lakes of Soma. One whole hymn (X.119) is a monologue in which Indra, intoxicated with Soma, boasts of his greatness and his might. His wife is Indrani. Indra is also associated with various other deities. The Maruts are his chief allies, who constantly help him in his conflicts. Agni is the God most often conjoined with him as a dual divinity. Indra is also coupled with Varun and Vayu, less often with Soma, Brahaspati, Pusan and Vishnu.

Generally, Indra is praised as the protector, helper and friend of his worshipers. He is described as bestowing on their wealth, which is considered the result of victories.

Besides the central myth of Vrtra fight, several minor stories are connected with Indra. In various passages, he is described as shattering the car of Usas, Goddess of dawn;

this trait is probably based on the notion of Indra's bringing the Sun when kept back by the delaying dawn.

The attributes of Indra are chiefly those of physical superiority and rule over the physical world. He is energetic and violent in action, an irresistible fighter, an inexhaustible lavisher of the highest goods on mankind. Some hymns are given below:

"O Indra! Owing to your sturdy and vistous physique, you are truly great. Let your voice always carry truth in a variety of all-engrossing ways and let it give us all that we desire. May Indra prove like a ripe fruit laden bow of a tree to the hast of the Yagya.

We hymn Indra, the protector of all wealth that we possess. O Indra! Be propitiated with our hymns and come to the *yagya* to imbibe with your share of the *Som Rasa*. Indra is an indispensable existence in the *yagya* who is all powerful.

May Indra eke out our all wants. May he give us wealth and wisdom. O Lord! Favour us in such a way as may prevent our enemies to cast a blow on us. May Indra satisfy men's all desires by his grace.

Indra, the lord of all wealth, please don't let us be involved in the sins and their consequences. Please cure our diseases and provide us the glory ever rampant. Make us wealthy and protect us. Nourish well our scholars.

O Indra! You alone are like a full army. You have huge wealth. Distribute it in such a way that we all get its even share. Let us also receive a part of that.

Indra! Make us devotees to the Sun, the water and to human beings. Please do not slay our child in the womb. We have faith in your power. The ancient sages have made you favour the *Soma Rasa*. Here lies the *Soma Rasa*, please drink it and oblige us.

May Indra, who imparts darkness due to dạwn (*Usha*) listen to our hymns created by the sages who existed before us. He who has appeared as the Sun on the heels of the dawn, Indra, may gratify us.

O Indra! Please ensure that rain and other disturbances do not create obstructions on our *yagya*. Let us all receive all things and commodities needed by a man. O Indra! Let you come as our nourisher."

Agni

Agni is the chosen priest, God, minister of sacrifice, the hotar, who lavishes wealth and dispels the darkness. No sacrifice is complete without his presence. His presence ensures the success of a sacrifice, because whatever sacrifice he accepts goes to the gods. Agni is the messenger, the herald, the master of all wealth, oblation bearer, much beloved, who brings the willing gods from the heavens and makes them sit on the grass with him near the sacrificial altar.

He is appointed by Manu as the priest. He is often invoked along with Indra, with whom he shares the passion for the *Soma* drink. He is also invoked along with Maruts probably to ward off the dangers of forest fires. Agni was the earliest Angiras, a seer. After his holy ordinance, the Maruts were born with their glittering spears. Agni is the lord of Red Steeds, who loves songs, kind and bountiful giver of gifts, of wondrous fame. Agni is the friend of all, loved by many in their homes.

The Vedic Aryans were well aware of his destructive ability, as he sets the forests aflame.

Some hymns dedicated to Agni have been given below:

Agni is the priest in the *yagya* and bears the fruits of the *yagya*. It is only through the grace of Agni that the host of the *yagya* gets riches and renown and all kinds of prosperity.

O Agni! Please incinerate our enemies and take our *yagya* to its culmination. Please take our honeyed oblation to the respective deities. Let these deities imbibe *Soma* through your tongue while making a typical sound.

O Agni! The nourisher of all the cereals fit to be used in *yagya*, you are robust and dazzling. We are hymning to you, please sit here and fulfil our desires and protect us.

May you bestow us with the cereals available in the divine realm and space and with the riches of the earth.

O Agni! You are yourself a God and friendly with other gods. It was your action that had bred the Maraudaganas. In order to shed your grace on the world, you manifest yourself in a variety of forms. You were born out of the contact of two Angiras. Grant the host all kinds of riches. Forgive us for the lapses that we might have committed in performing this *yagya*. O Agni! Please grant us wealth and protect us from our enemies.

O Agni! Start the process of performing the yagya with the association of the Vasus, the Rudras and the Adityas. Bring all the thirty-three divinities here. The hosts invoke you to come and accept the oblation.

When inspired by the winds, you burn trees. All animate and inanimate beings are scared of Agni. I request Agni to grant me wealth and protect me from all sins.

We desire receiving cereals from Agni lord with whom is permeated every action of men and gods and who is accessible only by intelligence. The way the king protects life in his kingdom, may Agni also be protective to us and do this noble act. O Agni, protect and nurture all the groups of beings having known the basic instinct of all men and gods. Let Agni be a chivalrous archer causing dreads in the hearts of the enemy and help us.

Agni is the master of the best of riches. It was by the grace of Agni that Sarama could get cow's milk from the Angiras.

O Agni! Please accept our hymns. You are like a brother to everyone and friendly to all. Let the *yagya* be completed for our sake, dedicated to Mitra, Varuna and other gods.

O Agni! Be our foremost leader! Please escort Indra to this *yagya*. Please be seated with other gods and play the role of the priest and the one who offers oblation.

O Agni! Please shine brilliantly so that we may come in wealth. Be pleased with our *sookta* and protect us.

O Agni, O Soma! Please accept our prayers and please us. Give the host cows and horses, sons and grandsons and full life. Please accept our service in the form of this oblation and dispel the fear of diseases from our mind.

As a carpenter carves out a chariot, the same way we carve out the reverential wisdom towards Agni and dedicate this well hymned *yagya* to him. May Mitra, Varuna, Aditi, oceans, Earth and welkin ensure that our enhanced age remains well protected.

Agni ever keeps his right hand ready to donate wealth to the one who performs the *yagya*.

O Adhvarya! Prepare the altar for depositing the oblation

for offering it to the Agni. Cover the place with beautiful *Kusha* grass.

Agni nourishes my body by providing heat to consume the ingested food. My wisdom only works when supported by the brilliance of Agni and achieves its objectives.

O Agni! Please ensure our welfare by appointing alert and agile guards to make us happy.

O Agni! You are omniscient. Please protect us by your rejuvenating rays which removed the blindness of Dheergatama. Please protect us by your same rays.

Agni dazzles with renewed radiance the moment the syllable 'Swaha' is pronounced.

O Agni! Please remove our sins which take us on the wicked path.

Agni! Protect us from our ill-wishers. Give me ample happiness and riches.

We see Agni being elevated to the status of a Supreme God.

Rudra

The Rudra of the Rigveda is a militant God of storms and lightening and a provider of medicines. Rudra enjoyed his own importance in the vedic pantheon because of his tempestuous nature, his association with storms and storm gods called Maruts and his ability to bring medicines to the people to prolong their lives.

He is a fierce-looking God, well built and golden in colour, with braided hair, of firm limbs, multiform, strong, tawny, who adorns himself with bright and gold decorations. He wields the thunder bolt, bow and arrow, and sends down streaks of lightening, shaking the worlds, making people nervous with fear and disturbing the cattle in the cow pens. Intelligent and benevolent, he protects people from their enemies.

May Aditi grant us and our progeny the herbal medicines related to Rudra. May all gods shed their grace upon us. We supplicate our desire before Rudra like the son of Brahaspati, shanyu, had done. Rudra has a bright shine as is possessed by the son. He is the best among the dieties. We are hymning Rudra so that all our disease, may be cured and all remain healthy and free from diseases. May Rudra provide herbal medicines with his own hands and grant us an armour of happiness and a good home to dwell in.

Mitra and Varuna

Mitra and Varuna are both lords of heaven. Together they uphold the law, cause the cows to stream, the plants to flourish and scattering swift drops send down the rain-flood. Both are Adityas and mostly are invoked together probably because of their close friendship.

Firmly set in heaven is Mitra's home and Aryaman's and Varuna's. Thence they give forth great vital strength which merits praise, high power of life that men shall praise. Both Mitra and Varuna are guardians of the world, who sit in a gold-hued chariot from day break and behold the infinity. In course of time, Mitra came to be associated with meaning light, while Varuna with night sky.

Vayu

Vayu is described in the Rigveda as beautiful God, ideally the first partaker of *soma* juice which he seems to be especially fond of. He is a friend of Indra and a hero who shares the glory of victory with the latter. He is swift as mind the thousand eyed and the lords of thought. He drives a chariot yoked with steeds, whose colour vary from red to purple and the number from two to hundreds and even thousands, depending upon the occasion. He is praised in the hymns as the intelligence who illumines the earth and heaven and makes the dawn to shine.

"O Wind God! Please come to our *yagya* and imbibe *soma rasa*. O wind, Indra is thy charioteer. May he also come here. May you come riding your golden chariot."

Surya

Surya is the blazing sun. He is one of the Adityas, God among gods, the light that is most excellent, golden coloured, who rides the skies in his golden chariot, drawn by seven bay horses, who are described in the hymns as the daughters of heaven. He is said to be extremely brilliant, with radiant hair, who flies in the skies like a bird and shines brightly like a jewel. He is a giver of power and strength.

O Sun God! Make us sinless amidst all the deities the moment you rise. The sun is the nourisher of all animate beings and the sole scrutinizer of all human sins and meritorious deeds. He with his power makes even the ignorant a scholar. He is also depicted as provider of good health.

Vishnu

Vishnu alone supports all the three material worlds: the earth, the sky and all the realms. Vishnu of the rigvedic times is one of the Adityas, but with some qualities of the Vishnu of Bhagvatism, He is a lover and protector of devotees. He is adorable by all hosts. They come close to Vishnu who offer you oblation every day. He grants us the desired wish and the delighter of the host's heart.

Savitr

Savitr is an Aditya who is described as golden eyed, golden handed and golden tongued. He is regarded as the sun before sunrise, but sometimes distinguished from the sun. He represents the golden sun of the morning as well as the hidden sun of the dark night also. Riding a golden chariot, he comes, looking on everyone. He is an upholder of law and forgiver of sinners.

Pusan

Pusan is the lord of the paths, who protects people from wild animals and makes their paths in solitary places pleasant to tread. He is a pastoral god. He is described variously as a cloud-born God, lord of the path, wonder worker, lord of prosperity and wielder of golden sword.

Pusan is the guardian of cattle who shows the way. He stirs our thoughts, drives away the enemies, inspires the miserly to make generous donations. In some hymns, he is also invoked along with Indra whom he helps to generate ripe warm milk from the young raw cows.

Usha

Usha is the dawn, the daughter of the sky, lady of the light, who rouses all life. She stirs all creatures that have feet, and makes the birds of air fly up. Borne on a hundred chariots, she yokes her steed before the arrival of the sun and is never late. Loved by the *asvins*, sister of gods, she eludes the sun who is always eager to catch her. She brings not just light to the sleeping mankind but hope, happiness, riches and all the good things. The hymns addressed to Usha in the vedas are among the most poetic and beautiful hymns.

For example...

"O daughter of heaven! Spread your glow. May the sun not scorn you. O Usha! You are capable of giving us all the riches whether expressly desired or not desired."

She comes before us like a bathed and decorated beautiful woman, like an auspicious woman she makes the oblation offerer happy.

Brahaspati

This God is addressed in eleven entire hymns and in two others conjointly with Indra. He is sharp horned and blue backed, golden coloured and ruddy. He is armed with bow and arrows and wields a golden hatchet or an iron axe. He has a car, drawn by ruddy streeds.

Parjanya

Parjanya is frequently described as a bull that quickens the planets and the earths. The shedding of rain is his most prominent characteristic. In this activity, he is associated with thunder and lightning. He also produces fertility in cows, mares and women when he pours down rains with a great roar, the whole world gets delighted. It is for the welfare of the world that Parjanya produced medicinal herbs.

Prithvi

O Earth! You bear all the beings and keep them happy. You only push away the roaring clouds. When the clouds pour rains upon you, you by your innate power produce medicinal herbs.

Asvins (Ashwini Kumars)

These two deities are the most prominent gods after Indra, Agni and Soma being invoked in more than fifty entire hymns and in parts of several others.

"O Ashwini Kumars! Please come to this *yagya* which ever realm you may be in. You both have stabilised one wheel of your chariot for stabilising the sun. May your protective endeavours keep us alive, we have carved these hymns like a carpenter carves the chariot. May you never lose the desire of helping us."

They are twins and inseparable. They are strong and agile, fleet as thought or as an eagle. They desire honey and are drinkers of it. They dispel darkness and chase away evil spirits.

Soma

As the soma sacrifice formed the centre of the ritual of the Rigveda, the God Soma is one of the prominent deities. With rather more than 120 hymns addressed to him, becomes next to Agni in importance.

The soma juice, which is intoxicating is frequently termed "*madhu*" or sweet draught. The colour of soma is brown, ruddy or more usually tawny. The juice passes through a wooden strainer, and flows into wooden vats in which it is offered to the gods on the letter of sacred grass.

Soma is regarded as a divine drink bestowing immortal life. Hence, it is called *Amrita* draught of immortality.

All the gods drink *soma*. It confers immortality not only on gods but also on men. It has moreover medicinal powers. Soma heals whatever is sick, making the blind to see and the lame to walk. Soma also stimulates the voice and awakens eager thoughts. He is a generator of hymns, a leader of poets, a seer among priests.

Funeral hymns

The Rigveda contains a group of five hymns connected with earth and then future life. From them we learn that though burial was also practised, cremation was the usual method of disposing of the dead and was the main source of mythology relating to future life. Agni conveys the corpse to the other world.

Saraswati

In the Rigvedic hymn addressed to Saraswati, she is depicted as a river of Goddess who slays the Parvathas with her might, casts down those who scorn the gods and makes poison flow away from the waters. She is the giver of strength and wealth. She has seven sisters, sprung from three-fold source, who is invoked in every deed of might and sought for treasures. Saraswati subsequently became a Goddess of learning. But in Rigveda she is river Goddess with seven sisters who helps the gods, destroys enemies and provides water to the five tribes.

Yajurveda

Yajurveda Samhita is known as the book of the *yajus* (sacrificial prayers). The *mantras* are meant to be chanted by a special class of priests called *adhavaryus* during sacrificial ceremonies. These hymns are addressed to various gods and goddesses. The recitation of these *mantras* is supposed to have been a deep spiritual impact on the aspirant.

The Yajurveda is characterised by its division into two collection of texts. The first is known the Taithiriya Samhita, also called Krishna or black Yajurveda. The second is Vajasaneyi Samhati also called Shukla or white Yajurveda. The earlier one is called Black because it is rather confused showing the colour prejudice that the ancient had in their midset. Shukla Yajurveda contains only the *mantras* and its brahmna portion is collected separately in the 'shatapath brahmana' as is well known, each of the four vedas consists of the Samhita and Brahmana.

Black yajurveda is a disorderly mixture of prose and chants and the white Yajurveda consists of only chants and contributed extensively by Sage Yajnavalkya. The black Yajurveda is considered to be older of the two and composed around 1200 B.C.

Yagya यज्ञ and *yajuh* यजु: words have been derived from "यज्ञ देवपूजा संगतिकरणदानेषु". The whole history of the development of vedic *karmkand* lies in "देवपूजा संगतिकरण and दान".

Yajurveda inspires human beings for doing *karma*. There are 1975 *mantras* in Yajurveda. In the first mantra of Yajurveda lies the order of doing *karma*.

देवो व सविता प्रार्थयतु श्रेष्ठतमाय कर्मणे।

In the second *mantra* of 40th chapter, importance of *karma* has been described.

कुर्वन्नेवेह कर्मणि ज्जिीविषेच्छतं समा।

A brief description of some of the verses of Yajurveda has been given below:

O Water! You irrigate this altar! O Kushas! You are the crown-tail of the *yagya*! O Altar! You are soft. I unfurl the mattress for having you seated on it. May these incense material be fully acceptable to lord supreme.

O Agni! Spread all around for universal welfare. Save me from my enemy's tricks and from poisoned food and water. This *ahuti* is particularly meant for Agni and Saraswati.

O great Agni! You are the bestower of all the wealth and prosperity. We make you brighter by pouring in more incense. I seek your indulgence and bright you so that the process of food-grain-creation may not be hampered. I bow to the gods with the hope that they will bestow their favour to see my *yagya* endeavour successfully reaching its culmination.

O Agni! You are the messenger as well as the *hota* of the *yagya*. May you protect sky and earth and they protect you.

Satisfied along with the duties by our *yagya* performance may Indra fulfil all our desires.

May Indra grant to the *hota* all divine and earthly affluences, fulfil his all desires and allow his wish to be fruitful. May hymned mother earth permit me to consume the offerings, I, in the form of Agni, may consume them.

O Savita! You are the object of this *yagya*. Protect this *yagya*, its host and myself. May the divinities be satisfied with this *yagya*. May Savita Dev not go against us.

May we be endowed with divine geow, milk and its other products, capable senses and peace giving actions and mind. May Twashta give us wealth and health.

O Sun! you are self-created, golden hued and covered with rays. Please give me some divine glow.

O Agni! You are present in entire earth and sky! O Earth! Since you deserve a *yagya* or your surface entirely. I establish Agni at the altar. Then like the space filled with planets and stars, may it also be filled with pure and dense smoke and become an eventual support to the earth. This Agni is entirely pure and he accomplishes only what is noble.

Agni is the veritable *hota* of every *yagya*. The Bhrigus, who knew all about the *yagya* rituals, had produced him in the forest for public welfare.

O Agni! By your nature you protect the body of the *yagya* performers. You also ensure our good health by remaining present as the digestive fire (*Jatharagni*) hence you must protect me as well and grant me full age and strength.

O cows! Since you are the fount of milk, you also get us food. May I ever enjoy milk given by you. Since you are the embodiment of all strength, may I become power also by your grace. Since you nurture us with providing wealth, may I become affluent by your grace as well.

Like a son easily receiving his father so, O Agni, we reach you. Please get us involved in the auspicious *yagya* work for our benefit.

Mitra, Aryama and Varuna are sons of Aditi. May they provide the host with brilliance and long age.

O Agni! You are very radiant. May you grat us illimitable wealth. May you come here with all wealth, food and power at your command and give us all these gifts.

O Agni! Give us money, wealth and power.

O Marudgana! You become delighted with the Sattoo and curd's mixture. O Sun destroyer, Marutas! We invoke you.

O Indra! You are supremely powerful, protect us with the Marudganas in the battlefield. Your share in the *yagya* oblation has been duly apportioned. We worship you and the Marudganas and offer you our salute.

O Indra! Be gracious on us, we hymn you. Please come here as you can fulfil our desires.

Shedding light on the three realms for punishing the sinners the soul force in the oblation separately as distinct for on that meant for the other gods. May Rudra endow us with the best of the dwelling place. Give us all that is best and keep us engaged in only noble deeds.

O Deities! The *yagya* has started. You must grace it with its fruitful consequences. We pray you to come with our desired fruits.

I give this offering to Agni with an ardent desire for the performance of the *yagya* "*Swaha*". This offering is meant for propitiating Saraswati, Poosha and Agni. O Water! You are pure, bright, great and give diligent to all. We give the offering for propitiating the sky and earth, space and Brihaspati.

O Ritwijas! This Agni represents three Vedas and it is the vital means to perform *yagya* in. May we receive the wisdom inspiring us to perform divine work. May this offering enhance the potency of our life force.

O Waters! May you prove salubrious to the stomach when you are drunk by me. These waters, nectareous, are queller of the diseases, the divine portion received by us for performing this *yagya*. May they ever prove tasty to us.

O Som! You are brilliant! I purchase you in exchange of gold. O seller of Som! I had given you cow and gold as the value of Som I purchased from you. May out of that bargain, the cow reach the host's place but gold may remain with you. O Som! With your grace I may get enough cattle, wealth and able progeny also.

O Agni! Remove the evil effects of my deeds and sins. Please re-establish me in a glorious position. May I get long age and ever keep following the divine examples.

O Agni! For ensuring our welfare you must come to your *yagya* shedding all lethargy. The offering of ghee is kept for you.

O Som! May Indra become stronger by imbibing you. Give us wealth and intelligence. May our welfare be assured. Our salutations to the earth and sky. May they have our endeavours duly completed.

O Earth! You are the mine of gems and jewels and the base for any agricultural endeavour, grant me desired affluence and protection.

Vishnu had divided this entire animate and inanimate world into three parts, the earth, the space and the sky. He did so by measuring the whole expanse by his steps. He whose one step covers the entire world has thus oblation dedicated to him.

O Earth and Sky! May you become endowed with many cows and ample food grains. O Vishnu! You have amazed us by dividing the earth, the sky and the space as separate entities.

O Vishnu! Use your both hands to dole out wealth to us from the earth, sky and space.

O lord of the world! You are omnipresent like wind carries Agni you make all material reach every bit of the universe. You are the fount which makes all beings conscious you are eminently honourable and extremely enlightening. Lord supreme is all-pervading. The whole universe is housed in his one foot's measure. He is the ultimate voice and abode of all.

Please make me cross the path of religion without any hindrance. Grant me happiness.

O Varuna! Ensure that we don't indulge in violence and sins. May all the water-borne medicines provide us safety and protection. May the host's this *yagya* get duly consummated with ample oblation, may the sun receive the oblation and grant this *yagya* in due reward to the *yagya* performer.

O Som! You are capable of raining down the fruits of our desires. Perfected by our hands may you enter this receptacle for the sake of Vachaspati Dev.

O Indra! You must protect this som kept in the pitcher and also our cattles and food assets.

O Indra! O Wind! This *yagya* is the place dedicated to you. O Som! I place you here so that you could gratify Indra and the wind God. O Mitra Varuna! It is for your gratification that som has been prepared you must come to this *yagya* to accept it.

O Mitra Varuna! Grant us the cow which is not available to anybody else.

O Ashwini twins! You must make your veridicious voice complete the rituals of this *yagya*. O Som! For the gratification of the Ashwini twins, I consecratedly establish you here.

O Planet! You have ample riches! Make the host endowed with much wealth and progeny. You are brilliant. You must enhance my life force, my voice force, my efficiency and my audition power as also my range of vision.

O Vishwadeva! You are our protector! You make men become strong. You must come to the host for imbibing som, I establish you here for ensuring your happiness.

O Agni! Guide us on the noble ways so that we may become affluent. Remove our sins emerging as the hurdles in our endeavours. We salute you and offer this oblation to you.

O Adityas! You are devoid of all the lethargy. You protect both men and gods. Your undecayable proficiency and blissful knowledge get their chivalrous vindication through the establishment of your realm's hallow.

O Indra! You are affluent. Give us a thoughtful mind, best of cows and other kinds of wealth. Make us accompany the best scholars and ensure our welfare.

O Gods! You have come here for enjoying oblation from this *yagya*. We have made your designated places entirely acceptable. You are present in every being. You carry the oblation, keeping it in your chariots. But those, who don't own a chariot, you should deliver their oblation unto them. Give us best of wealth. May this offering made for you prove fruitful. Swaha!

O Agni! Give wealth to the host and ultimate lustre to us. O brilliant Agni! May I also become brilliant by your grace.

O Supreme Lord! You make the devotees enlightened. You want to be adored and offered oblation. You are adorable for the ancient sages.

O Cows! May you ever remain satisfied with the host. Give him your affection and stay at his place. May this offering prove fruitful.

O Indra and Maruta! Take on the enemy desirous of fighting with us with your thunder bolt to subside him. May your thunder bolt get even the far-off positional enemy and tear him in twain. May we be blessed with the best of progeny and wealth by your grace.

O Lord! You have created Arya, Brahaspati, Indra, Saraswati, Vishnu and others. Inspire them to give us wealth and food. May this offering prove fruitful.

O Waters! You reside in the skin of the sun. Make me and the host with strength and authority. May the offerings made separately prove fruitful.

O Savita Dev! With a gold implement in his hand, raise Agni high from the earth with *anushthup* verse as did Angiras.

Agni! You have a fiery face. You remain quite for the sake of people. I dig the earth like Agni to get Agni from deep below.

O Couple! May you survive, happily. May you exploit all alight means and the electric fire produced by them enjoy all sort of their uses with wealth and contentment.

O Physicians! Well versed in your job! Keep my body free of diseases by using these thousands of medical herbs.

O Medicines! This land is your mother. Like the earth you protect us by destroying all our ailments. You must cure the people of the diseases.

These medicines kill all disease germs. They pervade the whole body to throw the afflictions out of it.

O Medicines! You protect the person from tubercular affliction the moment you enter his body.

First of all there emerged Prajapati as the Hiranyagarbha.

He wrought the heavens, space and the earth. It is for him that we offer oblation.

Prajapati then established Aditya, the original form of all creations who with his *sap* (light) satisfies all and move all over the three realms.

O Please-giving Woman! May all scholars praise you, and you get all noble wealth and education. May Ashwini Kumars establish you in the family stage.

May women get all happiness in the realm as well as wisdom. May they enter with their husband, adorned with best of ornaments, into their house.

Desirous of knowing the hymns, you have a good name with much of material at your disposal. May you be well established in the family stage by Ashwini Kumars.

O Self-sustaining Mother! You spread and remain instinct in all over the sky. May Vishwa Karma establish you in the space. May Wind God protect you. May you become as firm as Angira.

O Rudra! You repose on mountains or inside the rain laden clouds. You protect all beings to make your deluge causing voice auspicious for the world. May our men or cattle suffer no violence.

O Rudra! Spare all our kins and kith, our children, youth infants in the womb, our parents and our body from any kind of violence.

O Agni! May your flames torture our opponents. May your prove purges of the impieties and entirely auspicious for us.

As the reward of this *yagya*, may the divinities grant me food, piety, concentrating power, the resolution to listen to vedic teachings, light and the heaven.

May my energy and my tolerance my soul-power and

my body, my happiness and my armour, my thought and speech, my limbs and my bones, my joints and my members, my health and long life prosper by this sacrifice.

May my truth and my faith, my cattle and my wealth, my share and my greatness, my play and my pleasure, my son and my future, my hymn and my rites prosper by this sacrifice.

May the Maruts come unto us today. Let all guardian gods come our sacrifice to protect us. Let all the Agnis be kindled well. May we gain wealth and richness.

O Mauratas! You are the source of rain pouring down the earth and the blessing arising therefrom. May I attain you from all sides. May this offering prove fruitful.

O Agni! Grant glory to our Brahmanas set lustre in our Kshatriyas, lustre in our Vaishyas and in our Shudras and in me establish all lustre.

It is through Agni that law is upheld, truth is spoken, the earth is sustained, the foe is destroyed and the priests are protected. Agni also protect warrior classes.

O Omnipresent! You are placed at the head of the world, your heart is in the sea, your life is in the waters, guard us by giving us waters.

May Agni, satisfied with the oblation fulfil our desires. May this oblation quickly reach the gods.

May Agni, Vishwakarma's own establish us among the gods in heaven, where the streams of honey, milk and ghee flow ceaselessly.

Som is the best oblation, extremely pleasant for the sacrifices. Now o Ritwijas mix that duly processed som with cow's milk.

O Som! Since you enhance splendour, heroism. aggression, grant me the same. Grant me tolerance as *well.*

O Men! Be wise to study the properties of oblation, som, milk, crushed food grains and honey.

O Scholar! Chant the *strotas* and teach the students well so that they become learned and knowledgeable.

O Agni! You prolong life! Pour down on us food and vigorous strength. Drive you afar from us the gang of evil doers.

O Pavaman (wind god) you what is good or bad. Make me pure by divine influence.

O King! With best of wisdom, action and behaviour may you truthfully rule over unfettered kingdom. May we remain stable in our houses, protected by you.

O Truthful doer of the best deed and upholder of justice. May you prove to be very pleasant and bestower of all happiness to me.

O Man! My arms are strength and richness bestowing. Action and valour is what they are meant to display. May heart and soul protect the noble from grief.

O Planet! You are protector of my all vital breaths and winds, of my ears and eyes and my all senses. May you repose your influence in my voice, mind and the medicines that I take.

The sun that leads the dawn, in the form of Indra had slain Vritna to open the gates of the courts.

Saraswati and Bharti service Indra, may they fully fill our *yagya* with best kind of oblations.

May that hymned Indra come here for ensuring our protection and accept the oblation in the company of deities.

I invoke Indra! May he ensure our welfare.

May Indra be our protector, removing our misfortunes, may he grant us good luck, food, destroy our fears and make us rich.

O Ashwini Kumars! O Saraswati! Protect us day in and day out. O divine Hotas! Protect Indra when he is having prepared Som.

Saraswati, Indra, Bharti and Ashwini Kumars prepared Som with the help of medicines.

O Varuna! Hear this my prayer! Be ever gracious unto us; longing for help I yearn for you.

O Varuna, O Mitra! Your gracious pair sprinkle our pasturage with rich *sap*, and with honey the realms of the air.

Morning and night, the Goddess called upon Indra as the sacrifice began. May they well beloved. Our well-wishers make the divine subjects come here. May they enjoy oblation of ghee for enriching the sacrifice in wealth and position.

We call the gods here with hymns composed by our ancient fathers. We invoke Bhagadevta, the friendly Duksha, Mitra, Aditi, Arayman, Varuna, Som and the Ashwini Kumars. May auspicious Saraswati vouchsafe our wealth.

Come, O Agni, come to guard us from the distant land. Come Vaishvanara, to listen to our beautiful hymns of praise.

Agni has entered all, he has entered the sky, the earth, the air and the sun. May that Agni, pervading all, preserve us all day and night from harm.

Samveda

Samveda is the third of the collection of vedic *mantras*. It has 1875 verses or *mantras*, each of which has a specific metre. The text of each *mantra* of samveda is identical to the text of some *mantras* of Rigveda Samhita but the corresponding *mantras* of the two Samhitas differ in their notation and intonation.

Samveda Samhita is known as a book of chants. The hymns contained in this are more lyrical in nature and suggest to the early musical traditions of the vedic people samveda is the earliest known systematic procedure for giving melody to a chanted verse. Most persons, who have heard with devotion the singing of Samveda verses, well attest to the sense of exhilaration experienced by them. Each samvedic *mantra* contains in it not only the deep meaning of the counter part of the Rigvedic *mantra* but also has the added dimension of music. Samveda is the foundation for all systems of music in the subcontinent of India.

Samveda itself has three recentions namely Kouthumiya, Rahayaniya and Jaiminiya. The first two are identical in both text and intonation, they differ from each other only in grouping of the verses into *adhyayas,* etc. The Jaiminiya recension has fewer mantras, only 1693, but it has more *ganans* or final songs. Each chapter takes verses for different *mandals* of the Rigveda. For instance, the first ten *mantras* of the first *adhyaya* of Samveda having 11 *mantras* have same text as following Rigveda Samhita.

The hymns in Samveda are addressed to Indra, Agni, Mitra, Varuna and later on, partially to Vishnu as well, Usha has also attracted some choicest hymns. Perhaps those who composed hymns may have found dawn as the best tune for chanting in the entire day. In fact, these prayers are very ordinary and simple. All of them desire from the addressed divinity food, land, cattle, horses, wealth, progeny, prosperity, renown, affluence and adequate rains which may be the desire of any common man.

At times Indra becomes lord Almighty and at other times Agni is also addressed in the same way. Som is also enlogised in the most glowing terms. When it is ready, it is envinced with the mixture of milk, curds and ghee. Having perfected it, it is, amidst the chanting of the mantras, poured over brightly lit Agni from where in the form of fumes it rises to the sky to tempt the deities to come down to have it. When it reaches upto clouds, Indra makes the clouds shower rain. Rains are important for the survival of both human beings and to keep our animals sturdy. There are variations but this is what a sacrifice is all about.

A brief description of some of the verses of Samveda has been given below.

Agni grants enlightenment of knowledge, accepts all oblation to help the host invoke the divinities.

O Men! Hymn Agni who is your well wisher like a true friend. An extremely lovable entity, ever on move like a quest, placed at the moment at the holy altar, the vehicle of all the divinities.

O Agni! Please ensure all security to our *yagyas* that are performed to give us all pleasure. You are the light in our eyes through which we see everything.

O Agni! Taking the oblation cereals in the ladle of *yagya*, may we everyday reach near you.

O Agni! We invite you to visit this beautiful *yagya* venue for drinking som rasa. Please do come.

The sun shining with his fill glory in the sky, who keeps the day brightly lit for the entire duration, also has in its shine the basic element of Agni.

Brilliant and resplendent Agni, with his sharp radiance bewilders and neutralises all our violent foes. He is the granter of all affluence for us.

O Agni! You are great! You are accessible to those that desire to get into them the divinity virtuous.

Agni in the form of the sun destroys all darkness. It is his light which gives us heat, makes the wind blow and process of decomposition reaches its consummation. Hence, it also helps in curing all the diseases.

May all the divine powers given by Supreme Being cause happiness to us, gratify us fully and shower on us the desired pleasures.

O Agni great purifier! May you ensure a bumper crop of cereals to us the best of them! May you get us the best of water. Please grant us the righteous renown. May our all hymns reach Agni who grants all happiness to the host of the *yagya*.

O Agni! You reside in all the pieces of wood inherently, the *yagya* performers kindle you with the help of incense, then you become languorless and as much conscious as to take all the oblation offerings to the various gods. Then you take your due place among all the gods including the Wind God.

In order to ensure the prosperity to the performer of the *yagya*, we hymn Agni through oral prayers.

O Hymner! Propitiate Agni, so well renowned in the Vedas and whose glow spreads far and wide. With your hymns so that in return Agni grants us food, wealth and security. Agni is entirely capable to ensure your protection.

Agni in the form of lightening is spreading like Indra forceful all around heaven where Agni is duly established.

O Agni! May you be acceptable by all. You alone are the host, the oblation offerer, the purifier, the inspiration, the performers of the *yagya* and the carrier of the oblation to the desired destination.

May we make this virtuous Agni as fast moving as our chariot in this *yagya* and add to his strength.

This Agni at the venue of *yagya* sharpens our intellect. O Agni! May your grace never make us sad anymore.

O Agni! The learned scholars create you amidst the chanting of the vedic hymns in a variety of ways. You look like lightening blazing behind the mountain from the water laden clouds. The vedic hymns strengthens you through various prayers and then you win all the battles for us like the steed which follows every command given to it.

That Agni almost touches heavens with his high rising flames. It perpetrates into the clouds to make them thunder for showering down rains.

O Agni! You grant cow and other animals to those that constantly perform *yagya* to gratify you. You help them in their every pursuit and grant them food grains as well. May you grant us all these things the same way. May you help us, get progeny and may we get righteous wisdom by your grace.

Agni! You cause beneficial rains on the earth. You help us in seeing things. Are one of the vasus and like Mitra you mature this crops.

O Men! Pour in your highest offering into well-kindled Agni since by doing so you shall get a bumper crop of cereals.

You must know fully about that foe, destroyer men-friendly Agni who with all his glow is keeping all stars and planets well lit.

That man who offers oblation to Agni to be carried forth to the deities stands protected from all the deceit and conspiracies of the foes. They can't damage him.

O fast moving protector of the people, O Agni! Please incinerate my disturbing illusive foes immediately.

When lord almighty Agni shows his favour to his devotee's performance of a *yagya*, all the disturbing and wicked elements get automatically removed.

O performer of hundreds of deeds! O Supremely affluent Indra! Make us happy with your bliss giving renown.

May we strengthen Indra with that share of the *yagya's*

oblation so that he may cause plentiful rains here.

O Indra! You are famous for your power, potency and forbearance. You are an incomparable deity as far as the earth's irrigation with water be concerned.

O Indra! You love your devotees with the same intensity as shown by a pigeon to his pregnant wife. Since we are also your devotees, you must listen to our prayers.

O Indra! He who is protected by supremely knowledgeable Varuna, Mitra and Aryana is never killed.

O Indra! You must reach this *yagya* as well for granting is cows, horses, chariots, and reputed wealth as you have done in the earlier *yagya*.

O Indra! The daughter of the sun, Usha, dispels darkness as it appears. She guides men to tread only righteous path by its shining splendour. But she does so by your grace only.

O Usha! May we partake of our cereal only under your and the sun's glow.

We, the *yagya* performers seeks Indra's help for getting additional strength.

He, who offers oblation to the blazing Agni, gets the favour of Indra in the form of wealth and food.

O Indra and Agni! Please grant us a sturdy, fast horse and nourishing food so that we could offer you your desired oblation.

O Indra! Grant us food which you deem to be the best. May we become capable of receiving that best of food from you.

O Som! Give us light, happiness and all good fortune.

O Som! Give us strength and capacity to show it in destroying our enemies.

O Som! With your natural reaction and protection means take us to the land of action.

Please help us establish our superiority in all the battles that we fight in the war.

O Som! Make us receive that which serves our life's interest best and full long age.

Som, the food giver, is as dear to us as wealth. Som moves into the rain laden clouds and causes rains.

Just Mitra, the trounces of the enemies and Mitra are hymned by us in early morning.

O Mitra and Varuna, may we be devoted ever to you since with your grace we can get food and happiness.

May lord supreme remain ever qualified with us so that our people enjoy all wealth and food and share the same with us as well.

O Achiever of a hundred deeds! Grant wealth to all those *stotas* with such intelligence as could not be misused. Please fulfil their desires.

May we perform the *yagya* every day so that we may be spared of drought. We may do so as religiously every day as a cow is milked early in the morning.

O Lord Supreme! Please destroy the power of those that cause grief for men and destroy that foe who attacks us violently.

O extremely lighted, brilliant, rich and settler to all, Agni! Please become manifest before us to give us wealth.

May Indra procure for us the needed medicine from the sun rays and the winds.

When Som is extracted amidst the chanting of the hymns, it spreads its streams in every direction.

The lustrous Ritwijas as well versed in the right and Dharma ordained performance of *yagya* offer the oblation of Som into Agni.

Mitra and Varuna are superior to all the deities. They are

the origin of water and light so they should be collectively hymned.

He who religiously worships ever adorable and eminently indomitable Indra never gets affected by enemies blows.

O Indra! Grant us food which you deem to be the best. May we become capable of receiving that best food from you.

Som makes Indra radiant as it has the mind of the sages and it is extracted by them only which enlightens intelligent minds.

This Som enhances Indra's power and makes him shower rains to fulfil our desires.

O Som! You are being massaged with our ten fingers. The seven performers do the *havan* of you in the fire. Then these intelligent persons get strength from you.

May we consume Som, so good for our eyes and so happiness endower to Indra and get able progeny.

O Som! Cause rain on the earth to make it produce abundant food grains. Give us power to win the battle we fight.

O Som cause plentiful of rains so that we may get food and from it strength.

O purified Som! Give us lot of wealth so that our house may look graceful.

Som, drunk by Indra, destroys our enemies.

O radiant and pure Som! Grant us great wealth, kill our enemies and gratify us with blessing as with progeny and renown.

Indra is the bestower of food and wealth to us. He is extremely powerful. He is ever ready for drinking Som and he eminently deserves so.

O Som, granter of the divine attributes! You make the juice flow in vegetation due to the rains you cause by sustaining the world.

O Som! Shower happiness for the gods, space, the earth and its people.

O God! You are the creator, nectarious in form, most powerful and the sustainer of all the realms. Make us pure to dwell in the world offering a variety of endeavour while adhering to truth.

Indra, most adored in the vedas, the wielder of the thunderbolt, piercer of the rain laden clouds, very youthful and roaring, the performer of all the work with success, now appear in the *yagya*.

The Ritwijas perfect Som, the green hued potion through *yagya* for the sake of getting strength in return.

This Som helps in producing food grains and its accomplishments an ineffable.

Some accomplishes many jobs in the great divine endeavours.

This Som destroys the disturbing elements as it is capable of quelling their troubles, it is a scourage of the wicked.

Deligentfully extracted this Som gives the inspiration to the sun to cause rains.

That sage, who teaches these som-related aphorisms, gets by Goddess Saraswati's grace all best potions like milk, ghee and sweet water.

These hymns are very auspicious when they are reverentially recited. Men get all happiness and the feeling of immortality.

O Agni! You are distress dispeller and happiness enhancer, our dear friend. Those who had a very regimented life enhance your brilliance with their hymns. May the wealth you condescend to give us become enjoyable for us. Protect us like all the other gods.

May our hymns eulogising Som gratify Indra's heart the same way as mother's milk gratifies their children's heart.

They, who have Indra as their friend manage to defeat their enemies with the help of their power.

O Som! You gather yourself on the sieve for those wishing speedy completion of the *yagya* and this way Som destroys our sins. Please make us happy. May you flawless cover all waters.

O Indra! Protect us from fear of violence. Become capable of protecting us and kill our violent enemies.

Let us chant hymn for manifesting the Agni. May that Agni protect our wealth and our ministers and desist us from committing sin.

O Lighted Agni! Make your all properties which are beneficial to us and far moving be properly utilised.

May Agni having Som poured over it, emit white fumes to all diseases and afflictions of the world.

O Agni, granter of wisdom and vision to us, give us food, wealth and progeny and keep the sky well lit.

O men! Offer Som in the receptacles for mighty Indra's consumption.

If you offer freshly extracted juice to Indra, he may grant you all affluence. He is the wisest and mightiest who trounces the enemies in a trice.

O pure Som! Go with our supporter Indra and procure for us auspicious wealth.

May our voice chant sweet metered verses in the seven metres including the gayatri and may it be praised.

Atharvaveda

Atharvaveda is somewhat different from the other three vedas. The first three vedas deal with the gods and future life of man but Atharvaveda deals with the present life of a man, his practical problems, protection from the enemies, politics and his day-to-day welfare. Atharvaveda deserves our highest consideration and respect because it contains the large number of highly philosophic hymns. This veda is also called 'Brahmveda'.

Atharvaveda means the knowledge of Atharvas. Atharvas were a class of highly intellectual priests who are reputed to be the first to have instituted the fire worship. They are believed to be the earliest teachers of the Brahm Vidya.

Atharvaveda Samhita contains mostly magical chants which alludes to the growing influence of the native kings over the Aryan traditions. It deals with the Agmas and the Tantra literature. It contains several hymns highly intellectual and philosophical in their contents and significance. It deals mainly with the practical side of life, with man, his security and protection, destruction of the enemies, the use of magic charms and the herbs for removing diseases, evil omens, ill effects, evil spirits, anointing of kings, political affairs, marriages, funerals, welfare of the common man, etc.

Atharvaveda contains about 5977 *mantras* which are a mixture of prose and poetry, this Samhita is divided into 20 candas and about 75 hymns which are essentially spells, marriage and burial songs and curses. Atharvaveda Samhita is the oldest document of the Indian medicine and magical formulas to deal with the diseases and sickness. The priests who chanted these hymns were prized by the royalty for their special ability to cure diseases and drive away the evil spirits or curse their enemies.

O Vacnaspati Brahma! Please establish my wisdom in affluence. Make us ever full of knowledge.

May water full of all the divine qualities give us happiness and pleasure.

O Brahaspati! Please destroy this demon seeking your shelter suffering distress from you only. Become strong by the charge of the *mantra* and destroy this demon's entire life.

May Varuna, Surya, Agni, Vasu, Indra, Pousha and other deities grant enough health and other resources to the *yajaman* and may Aditya and Vishwadeva make him illustrious.

Varuna Dev is the controller of all and has the authority to punish the sinners. He is capable of speaking the truth. Gaining strength from him I have become strong and in this capacity I endeavour to protect the host troubles by wrath of Varuna. O Varuna! May this host, now devoted to you live for hundred years.

I am performing the *yagya* with milk, ghee and other oblation to satisfy the deities. May they also remain favourable to me. May all rivers, winds and bords remain ever favourable to me. May we get ghee, water, cattle-wealth and other resources to our heart's desire.

May all the gods including Indra and sun ever remain our friends. May they provide us all happiness and good health and destroy all the afflictions.

O Vishwadeva, Indra, Vasuganas, Dhata, Aryana gods! Protect the host and make his enemies lose their strength. May no one be able to cause him any violence. O gods! Please ensure the host getting a long life.

Surya is the master of this world and hence adorable by all people. O Surya! While offering you the oblation I salute you. May he grant us all the happiness.

O sun ray adjoining with the rays of the moon. I also salute you while offering oblation.

O Agni! May you shine with your bright and beautiful flames and illumine the four quarters. O Agni! Let not thy devotees suffer, let thy worshippers be famed.

O Agni! You are the giver of life. Having enjoyed the

sweet pleasant ghee of the cow, you must protect this boy as a father does his son. Please put him in splendid garments, nourish him well to make him survive till ripe old age. Brihaspati, the guardian of the learned has furnished this garment Soma for wearing.

O Life breath! (Pran) May you be beyond the worries for death and be as eternal as the earth and sky. Be you redeemed totally of the fear of death like day and night stay away from apprehensions. May you be overlasting like the sun and the moon. May you face truth and untruth, present and future, with total quality.

O Wind! Let your wrath trouble those that are our enemies or whom we deem enemy. Radiant with you flame, show your wrath against our foes.

O Moon! Cause distress to our enemies and make them totally powerless.

O Water lord! Activate your affliction causing power and cause distress to our enemies and make them totally powerless.

May my all animals remain with me healthy and sound. May my progeny become strong with having lots of ghee and other nourishing material.

O herb called Patha! Keep my all the three bodily humours in check. I place you too reverentially on my arm like Indra did on his left arm and defeated the demons. You must ensure defeat to my opponents.

O Agni! May this child be cured of the disease and become healthy once again. Please make sure that no wind of the body ever disturbs this boy. May he never face violence from either the friends or the foes. O child! May the father sky and mother earth ensure your crossing even your old age happily.

O Wife! May you always love me and never go away from me. O Ashwini Kumars! May you fulfil my every wish and may my prayer reach unto you like a swift arrow reaches its target. I have come to my wife with all the wealth under my control.

May all the rays of the sun destroy the germs.

May lord Pashupati come to my this *yagya* and with his grace I get money and power. May God release all the rural animals which though different look alike.

O Indra! Disturb the enemies mind and incinerate them with the help of Agni and Vaayu. Infatuate them with your powers and enervate their determination to take on us. O Goddess of sin, Apva!

Permeate in the body of the enemies. Confuse and cause them much affliction to destroy them with their 'Moha-Pishaachee Vidya'.

The gods had made this gem Palashmani embedded in the Palash plant. May this gem also grant me power and wealth and long age.

May the horn of a dark deer remove the acquired or inherited deadly diseases like leprosy and tuberculosis. May the horn also cure other minor ailments.

May all the deities keep us healthy during the change of season and make us enjoy a long age.

May the nature grant us milk and best of fruits. May it prove totally auspicious for us. O night! Make our progeny long aged and we endowed with much wealth.

O Agni become happy by receiving our oblation and grant us all the seven varieties of cattle.

Waters grant us undecayable vitality and strength. Proper use of water keeps man conscious, vocal and endowed with all sensory perceptions and he enjoys his life blissfully.

May the indomitable brilliance coming out of the body of Aditi enter one. May Mitra-Varuna-Indra make me brilliant.

O Gwadharvas! You are capable of protecting me. Please grant me happiness and keep snakes and scorpious away from me.

O Cow! Producing twins make the host rich and prosperous in every way and prove auspicious to all the noble persons.

May the sun and his wife provide us with best of strength. May Prajapati keep our private part strong and healthy. O Agni, Sun, Brihaspati! Fill this man's body with manly vigour.

The first horn were these brahma with ten heads (symbolical) (charity, nobility, forgiveness, manly vigour, concentrating power, growth, forceful and many schemes to serve their end) who control all the ten directions. They drank the som and leaved how to detoxify poisonous tip get detoxified. O Poison! May my incantation take out all your toxic effects.

The Anwan bull, like Lord Almighty is the protector of the earth and sky, the space and the source of directions and perception. It is like Indra who sustains the world both animate and inanimate by showering rains while this bull produces the cows with its seed. The bull, like the sun moves all over the world to keep it lighted.

O Rohini! You are quite capable to heal up the wounds and hence you must stop bleeding in the wounds. May this Atharva Mantra set right the mutilated body parts.

May winds move speedily, lightening spark and the clouds gather to hide the sun. May those Agni rain nectarious waters to rejuvenate the entire creation.

O sky and earth! You grant affluence to men and gods. You are the bestower of wealth and entirely auspicious for all beings. You carry oblation to the desired destination. Make the rivers flow and the nourishes of cows and vegetation.

May Bhava-Sharva (Lord Shiv), whose weapons are inescapable for any, redeem us from all sins. May he cast his deadly weapon upon our enemy and protect us from sins. I hymn you with great devotion.

I am Brahma-Vadini (Goddess Saraswati) I roam about in the form of 2 Rudras, 8 Vasus, 12 Adityas and the Vishwadevas. I nourish Mitra, Varuna, Indra, Agni and Ashwini Kumars. I lord over the world.

O Manyu! You are the deity of enthusiasm and as powerfully moving as the marudgana. Become as brilliant as to overpower the enemy, of to the war and destroy the enemy and grant me wealth, power and protection.

O Manyu (the deity of anger) your assistants are as powerful as you are. You are the slayer of unfriendly, remover of all sorrow; bedlight in every awakened soul and supremely wise.

Destroy the enemy and grant me power during war time. I give you the som offering.

O Agni! In order to get a beautiful path and space in this world, we propitiate you with the oblation. I and my sons may be endowed with very able progeny. Save us from all sins.

May Agni give us food, wealth and a hundred year long life. May our enemies in south get destroyed by going close to Yama.

O Indra! You are linked to every being's intellect. You create taste in all edibles. It is by your grace that we are able to defeat the enemies.

The vegetation 'koot' produced on the Himalayas can cure most dreadful diseases. In the third firmament the gods have made this vegetation. May 'koot' endowed with the divine qualities cure all the diseases of head, eyes and other minor ailments.

The sun is my eyes, wind vitals breath, space soul and the earth is my body. May the sky and earth enhance the efficacy of my doings and protect us.

O my home! May he, who tries to destroy through you me from any direction be destroyed himself. I request power of eye from the sun, region from space, body from the earth and voice from Saraswati.

O Snake! I bind your sight with my gaze your poison cannot show any effect. It is ineffective like a she-snake dwelling in the tree of gular.

O Medicine! Make me sweet tongued.

O Indra! You are the lord of the universe. Delighted with som drinking, destroy my enemies.

May Twashtha, clouds, Brahmanaspati, Aditi, Bhaga, Mitra, Varuna and wind – listen to our prayers and ensure our protection from our violent enemies.

O Death! I salute you for ensuring protection of the king, Vaistiyas, duties from the deadly weapons. I salute to your messengers, your favour, the discreationary wisdom, your protecting herbal medicines and the torturing demons.

O Woman! May your embryo, like the earth, stays upto the entire pregnancy period unharmed.

O Jealous! We take you away from all anger and frustration by removing your jealousy.

May all the deities, men, all beings the som pressed and processed through the strainer - all should purify me, may Savita and som keep me pure.

May the flowing waters redeem us from the mess of sins. Inspired by the sun, may men perform the *yagyas*.

May all types of goitre be cured by the treatment.

We offer our salutations to Yama. O Deity! In order to escape tortures we offer your oblation.

O Shami! (tree) The juice of your stems is conductive to the growth of hair. May you grow every day and prove beneficial to our hair.

O Dream! Neither you are alive nor dead but get your affluence from the experience of the conscious state. Varuna couple constitutes your parents and your name is 'Araroo'. O deity of Dream! Spare us from nightmares, we transmit this dread for nightmares to our enemies.

May the cause of nightmares kept at bay by the grace of Agni. O Lord of Mantras! O Brahmanaspati! O Indra! Make Varuna destroy these nightmares dread and let Varuna destroy this sin.

O Ashwini Kumars! You must destroy the mice that eat up our cereals. O mice! Whether wild or tamed, we destroy you through our this sacrifice.

May the rays of the sun rising in the east grant this girl a husband and this man a wife.

We cause the downfall of the troubling enemy through our *mantra* power. Pleased with our oblation offering O Vritra slayer Indra, may you send my enemy down the oblivion so that he could never return.

O Agni! You destroy pregnancy destroying disease and demons. You must spread the ovary and O woman! you must conceive a son. May this woman deliver a healthy son.

O Horse! Get yoked in the chariot. May Marudgana make you move as fast as the mind. May you score over the opposing wind force. May you move smoothly till you reach the village and town.

O Agni! May Durva grass continue to grow before and behind you, near a pond full of lotus flowers. O Agni! Please never let your flames burn in the backward direction. O Chamber! May you remain ever strong, covering you with cold water course we place Shaivadl around you.

O Dundubhi! Fill the sky space with your sound so that you are heard by many. May you with Indra and Maruta, kill my enemies. Win over the air-borne forces.

I remove your influence O Kaam that shows all over my body. Keep this kaam away. O Lord Almighty! Make kaam not influence us.

O Mother Goddess! Remove the demons from the ocean and make the gods get their due right.

O Saraswati! Peace and happiness bestowing, pure, nourisher to all and entirely adorable, make us suck your breast.

May by the electric power generated by you the people be not be troubled.

O Savita! Please nullify the affliction carried by my host by sleeping at the sunrise time and make him determined and successful.

We forsake the evil dreams, a life full of distress, poverty, fear, of wrong pronunciation and of speaking lies.

May all the instruments to cut tress prove of much use and benefit to our host.

O Wife! May your mind and eyes ever have sweet feelings for me and you may carry my image in your heart.

With my mantras I invoke Raka (full moon night). May she listen to our hymns and after allowing us a safe conception, grant us a sow. May she grant us wisdom and wealth.

We employ the Rika and Saam Vedas through our

Ritwijas to hold the *yagya*. These two help our oblations reach the desired deities. My veda knowledge may grant me desired fruits milk out in any way damaging me.

O Dharba (grass)! May you spread upon the altar. This green seat is meant for the hotas. May this become gold-plated.

O Bull! Carrying Som! Populate this world. May my host's issues remain ever happy.

Water in different forms remain in this earth, sky and space. May they keep us safe from all sins.

O God of Death! We offer our prayers to you through these hymns. O Desirous of long age, may your vital breath and life stay in your body. May you escape the death noose so that you may not be deprived of the *darshan* of luminaries. May the wind in space prove pleasant for you and water nectarious. Come to light from darkness. May you not become the morsel of Yama's dogs. May not your kith and kin get any occasion to shed their tears on your demise. May all the gods ever protect you and your family.

This gem from the Tilak tree is the destroyer of evil Krityas of the enemies. This is going to be tied in my arm on the amulet. He who carries this gem remains safe from the attack of demigods. May the gem protect me and make me and my host survive for a hundred years in the pink of health.

In the beginning Brahma created earth from his stomach, sky from the back, space from the middle portion, directions from the ribs and prosperity from the pelvic region. The eyes generated truth and veracity, head the cosmic person and objectivity from the life breath.

This world is the creation of Supreme Being. He created every being, animate and inanimate world. He is the manifest in all the eight direction. He who knows him is called Purush.

O Waters! Give all deities their due share and establish us amidst the best and radiant water.

This heaven bestowing and enemy destroying cow in Indra's gift. May she close the violent mouth of the enemies.

O Bhava! O Lord of the beasts! Grant us the happiness. We salute you from every side. Use your weapons against the gods opponents. Kill the wild beasts. May we stay fearless by the grace of the army of Rudra.

The whole world is the product of Prana. It causes rain to get us food. The fire element created body rises up due to Pranavritti.

May I ever have this Pran ruling all over the world.

Nothing in the universe is a waste and everything has its utility. I hymn that I may be benefitted by all these noble endeavours.

May the earth spread wide to provide us joy, crops and food in abundance. O Earth! Thy snow-clad mountains, thy forests, thy oceans, thy rivers, be pleasant to us. May we remain disease free, long-aged and well-established in our welfare. O Earth, we give you oblation.

The cow Vashu manifests on the earth for the sake of Brahmanas. Donating such a cow to Brahmanas is a way of ensuring his own welfare. He who performs Swadha *yagya* for the departed ancestors, divine *yagya* to propitiate the deities and donation of Vashu to Brahmana gets beyond any scope of damage.

O Sun! hidden in space, rise up! Let you grace this world invoked with truthful and pleasant voice. May sun make the food hidden in waters emerge out and strengthen the beings of this world.

This sun, who blazes forth shining and covers the sky with his brilliance, also represents, Dhata-Vidhata, sky-earth, Aryama, Varuna, Rudradeva, Mahadeva, Agni and Yam. Marutas are his assistants and Indra gets light from him.

The gods made Rudra the guardian of the *Ishaan* direction. The rest of the diagonal directions guardians were made Sharva, Pashupati and Mahadeva.

O Waters! Touch my skin with your auspicious part. May our all organs get strength with this pure water. May it revive our body with strength.

O Medicines! Make my voice sweet and grant me concentration to keep my slushes under control. May my ears always listen to auspicious talks and my sight remain as sharp as that of Garuda.

May I ever enjoy best of time right from dawn to dusk and best of waters endowed with all the best virtues. May Varuna strengthen my vital breaths and Agni keep my strength well nourished.

O nightmare produced by Brahma-Pishaaci (a deadly -hell-hound) you almost cause my death. You are a veritable death. We know of your origin you are daughter Bharati and the extension of Yama's form.

May we remain sin free, get victory and land and the dread of a nightmare should vanish from our mind. O Power of Mantra! May this dread be transferred to these who carry ill-will for us to our enemies.

I put all the nightmares into the jaws of all consuming Vaishnawas. We remove our rivals far away from the heaven and sky. May all the consequences of my evil deeds done knowingly or unknowingly be destroyed by the gods grace.

O Sun! you make your rays scatter all over the universe

and keep it lighted. Please make us rich with cattle, wealth, establish us in the heaven and make us best among the visible and invisible beings. Make us unharmed by any sort of violence. I pray you to make me as much lighted as you are.

I make my friend Yama ever favourable to me. O Yama! Your glory resounds every realm. May you ever remain radiant with glory.

The share of Yama in the som-juice is being offered to him. Agni gets to the oblation as its carrier. O hosts! Give ghee offering for or yama.

O Preta (dead body's soul)! You are now going heaven wards. May you reach the manes safely with the she dog named Sarana's sons. O Manes! Provide this soul a sage place in your realm. The long nosed death messengers may re-establish life in our body.

O Preta! May you be received by all the manes whether surfeited with som or honey or not.

O Earth, the alter for the crematorium of this body! Give this dead man all post mortem comforts. May he get the rewards of all the *yagyas* that he had performed when he was alive.

O Lord of all, the ruler of the three realms, master of all wealth, make me enough affluent through my these hymns to make this earth prosperous.

May all the Nakshatras-king Krithika, Rohini, Mrigshira, Aadra, Punarvasu, Pushpa, Aashlesha, Magha, Poorya, Uttaraphalgunis, Hasta, Chitra, Swati, Anuradha, Jyeshtha, Sharvan, Dhrmishtha, Revati, Ashwini-Bharani- ensure my welfare, give us truthful voice and make us fortunate.

O Shining Koot (root with medicinal qualities) born at the Himalayas, torture the rascal and protect us. Even the chanting of its name protects the chanter from all fatal diseases.

O Indra! Come to this *yagya* astride your green horses and drink this som will pressed between the stones and tastefully processed. May our hymns draw you close to us. May you grace this *yagya* repeatedly.

❐

PURANS

2
Purans

Puranas are composed by Ved Vyas, the narrator of the Mahabharta epic. Being in Sanskrit, the Puranas are not directly accessible to the common people, however, they are available in vernacular translations. The Puranas contain the essence of the Vedas and are the sacred texts of Hinduism. They were written to generate devotion to God. The Puranas generally contain matters of religion, customs, ceremonies, sacrifices, festivals, duties of the various castes, different types of donations, details of the construction of the temples and images and description of the places of pilgrimages. There is an emphasis on the worship of Brahma – the creator, Vishnu – the preserver, Shiva – the destroyer, Surya – the Sun God, Ganesha – to keep away obstructions and Shakti – the Goddess. The Puranas are the texts that represent the Indian culture, civilization, history and geography. They are classified as Mahapurans and Upapuranas. The eighteen Mahapuranas have four lakh *shlokas*, they are not equal in length. The longest purana is the Skanda Purana and the shortest is the Markandaya Purana. There are eighteen major Puranas (which are known as Mahapurans), the details of which are as follows –

Brahman Purana

It has references of the stories of Brahma, Vishnu and Shiva and their worship. It includes many chapters related to Surya or Sun God, cosmology, mythology, genealogy, temples and pilgrimages, Sanskara, Dharmasastra, Yoga, Hindu philosophy and other topics.

Padma Purana

This purana is one of the eighteen major puranas.The text includes sections on cosmology, mythology, genealogy, geography, rivers and seasons, temples and pilgrimages like Brahma temple in Puskar, yoga,Atman (soul) Moksha and other topics. It has parts/khands, which are ;

(1) *Srishti Khanda* – It contains dialoge between Bhishma and the sage Pulastya and also the description of Pushkara, a famous place of pilgrimage.

(2) *Bhumi Khanda* – It gives decription of Bhumi (earth) and the tales of kings like Prithu and other sages.

(3) *Svarga Khanda* – It gives significance and importance of holy places including mountains and rivers.

(4) *Patala Khanda* – It narrates the life story of Rama, an avatar of Vishnu and also the life and deeds of Lord Krishna.

(5) *Uttara Khanda* – Presents metaphysical aspects of religion in a form of dialogue between Shiva and Paravati.

(6) *Adi Khanda* – Deals with the origion of world and also the importance of Brahma – The Creator.

Vishnu Purana

It primarily centres around Vishnu and His Avatars such as, Krishna, but it praises Bhahma and Shiva asserting that they are one with Vishnu. The Purana illustrates the story of sagarmanthan, stories of Dhruva, Prithu, Surya, Yama, Lord Krishna etc.

Shiva Purana

It conceives Shiva as the eternal principle – The Supreme God and the Cosmic soul. It describes stories of Lord Shivain details along with the glory of Shivas linage, an image of Lord Shiva. The Jyotislingas are -Malikarjuna in Andhra Pradesh; Somnath and Nageshvera in Gujarat;Vaidyanath in Jharkhand; Mahakaleshwar and Omkareshwar in Madhya Pradesh;Bhimashanker,Trimbakeshwar and Grishneshwar in Maharashtra; Kedarnath and Kashi Vishnanath in Uttar Pradesh.

Bhagavata Purana

It is a Mahapurana which relates to the incarnation of Vishnu, particularly of Krishna and his life. It preaches bhakti and emphasis on achieving moksha through cultivating a personal relationship with Vishnu in the form of Krishna. The teachings of Bhagvata includes several traditions, teaches dharma, yoga etc.

Narada Purana

This purana is a mahapurana and in two parts

(1) Purva part includes origin of universe,salvation, training of mantras,worship,rituals and the results of various fasts observed on particular days in

particular months.

(2) Uttar part contains beautiful tales of various incarnation of Vishnu, significance of pilgrimages. This purana is known as Narada purana because it was originally recited by the sage Narada. It is in the form of narration with dialogues between the sage Narada and Sanat Kumara – one of the sons of Brahma, wherein Narada explains the major places of pilgrimages, their locations and significance.

Markandaya Purana

It presents its yoga philosophy and asserts that it is the path to gain self knowledge and liberation(moksha) and thereby overcoming past karma. It contains some illustrations from Durga Saptashati – the story of destruction of demons by Goddess Durga and the various forms of worship in order to achieve desires.

Agni Purana

It contains descriptioins and details of various incarnation of Vishnu, about Rama, Krishna, Prithvi and the stars. It has pronounced the supremacy of Brahmana as a caste . It contains forms of worship, images, places of pilgrimagaes, funeral ceremonies, penances, medicines, omens, astrology and economics veterinary sciences, cosmology, history, law, martial art and a list of various weapons which were made of Dadhicha's bones to defeat the Vritra Asura.

Bhavishya Purana

The word Bhavishya means "to be" ; "will be" means – oracles and prophecies about the future i.e. astrological predictions. It consists of a list of royal dynasties of the predictions. It consists of a list of royal dynasties of the past which are followed by lists of Kings predicted to rule in the future. This purana also describes the worshhippers of Surya who were called Magas. They used to cook their meal for the sake of the Sun and eat only after praying to the Sun. There is also a reference to Shamba- the son of Lord Krishna and Jambavati. He constructed a Sun temple on the banks of river Chandrabhaga – Chenab. It also includes methods of worshipping Brahma, Ganesha, Skanda and Naga. It also describes festivals related to various Hindu Gods and Goddesses and their Tithis(dates), as well as mythology and discussion of Dharma particularly Vrata(vow) and Dana(charity), geography, travel guides and pilgrimages to holy sites.

Brahmavaivarta Purana

This purana is divided into four parts which are –

(1) Brahma Khanda deals with creation of Universe .

(2) Prakriti Khanda describes the nature of Gods and Goddesses and the ways they should be worshipped. It also throws light on heaven and hell and the cures for different diseases.

(3) Ganesh Khanda relates to the birth of Ganesha, hymns to him and his conversation with the sage Bhrigu.

(4) Krishna Janma Khanda relates to Krishna's birth and deeds.

Linga Purana

It describes glory and incarnations of Shiva and its

pilgrimages like the holy cities of Varanasi, Kedarnath, Prayag and Kurukshetra. Preaching about the greatness of Lord Shiva and propogation of Linga Puja are main objectives of this Purana.

Varaha Purana

It deals with the Varaha boar, the incarnation of Vishnu who narrated it as a boar to Prithvi – the Earth. It narrates the rescue of Prithvi, holy places and mantras. It however describes the glory of Mathura at great length as Vishnu incarnated himself as Krishna in Mathura. Its holiness is considered greater than of Prayaga, Puskara, Varanasi etc.

Skanda Purana

There are seven Khanda to this purana which are –

(1) Maheshwara Khanda – relating to Shiva.

(2) Vishnu Khanda – the part relating to Vishnu.

(3) Brahma Khanda – relating to Brahma.

(4) Kashi Khanda – relating to the old city of Kashi/ Varanasi.

(5) Avanti Khanda – relating to the kingdom of Avanti.

(6) Nagara Khanda – relating to the cities.

(7) Prabhasa Khanda – relating to the holy places.

It is mainly devoted to the life and deeds of Kartikeya, son of Shiva and Paravati. It contains number of legends about Shiva and the holy places associated with him and describes the different kinds of Patala – the underworld and the narakas – the hell. It also describes four eras – Stya yuga, Treata yuga, Dwapara yuga and Kalyuga. This purana also includes the self immolation of Sati, where she saw that her father had not kept Shiva's share in the yagya while the shares of other deities were kept, churning of the ocean resulted into emergence of many things like Chandrama, Kalpa tree, Lakshmi, poison, ambrosia etc.

Vamana Purana

This purana is devoted to tales of Vamana(dwarf) avatar of Vishnu. The purana describes the various tirthas – places of pilgrimages like Kurukshetra and Varanasi, the destruction of Daksha's yajna, Pralada – Narayana war, Goddesses Durga, her war with Shumbha, Nishumba and Mahishasura.

Kurma Purana

The purana describes the details of Kurma – incarnation of Vishnu as tortoise. It is narrated by Lord Vishnu to Narada. It describes the creation of Universe, the periodical process of destruction and recreation, the history of Solar – Surya dynasty and Lunar – Chandra dynasty, royal genealogies and the different eras. It also tells about yoga, glories of lingas, places of pilgrimages, virtues of Ganga, Yamuna and the city of Pragya, Karna yoga in Gita, daily duties, donation of alms, four ashrams(stages of life)repentness etc.

Matsaya Purana

The word Matsya means fish and the purana was first restricted by Vishnu himself in his incarnation of a fish to Manu. Lord Vishnu had taken the avatar of Matsya to save the seeds of all lives and Manu. It describes the places of pilgrimages, its geographical local and astronomical details, lists of lineages of various sages like Bhrigu, Angira, Atri, Vishwamitra, Kashyaya, Vashishta, Parashara and Agastya. It contains tales of Chandra, Surya and Kuru Vansh, description of Kalpa and yogas, tales of Savitri and Satyavan, results of auspicious and inauspicious motion of planets, birth of Parvati and her wedding with Shiva, birth of Kartikeya, duties of a king, creation of Universe, war between the demons and Gods and the churning of the ocean, donations etc.

Garuda Purana

The purana is divided into two parts viz – purva khand which discusses wide range of topics associated with life and living and the Uttara Khand which deals with rituals associated with death and cremation. This purana is in the form of instructions given by Vishnu to his carrier Garuda – the king of birds. It has sections on technique of praying Surya – the Sun God, Lakshmi – the Goddess of wealth and Vishnu. The cosmology in this purana revolves around Vishnu and Lakshmi and it is their creation that created the Universe. It also describes different types of Shalagrama images, Ramayana – the story of Rama and Sita, Gitasar, astronomy and astrology, physiognomy – the nature of men and women by their characterstics, jewels, tirthas like Hardware, Pragaya, Gangasagar etc, Vratas – special religious rites performed in a specific month where a nakshatra is in the sky or on a particular tithi, ayurveda medicines for a various diseases like fever, vomitting, loss of appetite, laziness, headaches, sweating, thirst etc, the art of taking care of horses and elephants. Some of the hindus read this purana while cremating the bodies of the dead. The mantras are chanted so that the ancestors are freed from all sins.

Brahmanda Purana

It deals with the origin of Universe as told by Brahma. There are stories about Shiva and Shakti i.e. Sati/Parvati includes an account of Daksha's yajna, the arrival of Sati and her immolation, creation of Virabhadra by Shiva who destroyed the yajna, churning of the ocean by Gods and demons and the emergence of poison, Shiva drank it and the poison made his throat blue and he became Nila – Kantha. There are references of war between Bhandasura and Lalitha Devi, an avatar of Parvati and her final triumph. ❒

UPANISHADS

3
Upanishads

The word Upanishad is derived from the word Upa (near) *ni* (down) *s*(h) *ad* (to sit), i.e. sitting down near. Groups of pupils sit near the teacher to learn from him the secret doctrine – the *Brahma* knowledge by which ignorance is destroyed.

The Vedas, apart from the hymn – *mantras* or the Samhita portion, also have three layers of commentaries integrally incorporated within, these are – (1) the *Brahma* – which contains prose commentaries on the rituals, (2) the *Aranyakas* – which contains the mystical explanations of the *mantras,* and (3) Upanishads – which contain highly philosophical and metaphysical writings about the nature of and the relationship between the soul and the Brahman. In fact, the Upanishads frequently cite the *mantras'* texts to give authority to what they teach.

The Upanishads were originally called Vedanta which literally are the conclusion to the Vedas. In the Upanishads, views about the Brahman (the Absolute or God) and *Atman* (one's true self) are discussed. The Vedas are the sturdy tree on which blossom the fragrant Upanishads.

Every Vedas has its own Upanishads. As per *Muktikopanishad*, there is a list of 108 upanishads, of which the prime Upanishads are – Isha Upanishad, Kena Upanishad,

Kathopanishad, Prasna Upanishad, Mundakapanishad, Taittiriya Upanishad, Aitareya Upanishad, Svetasvatara Upanishad, Chandogya Upanishad, Brihadaranyaka Upanishad.

Isha Upanishad: Isha means "Lord" – the Lord encloses all the moves in the world – that enjoyment be found by renouncing the world and not conveting the possession of others. It concludes with a prayer to the Sun and Agni. It is significant for its description of the nature of Supreme being. It presents a non-dual perspective of the Universe. For the enlightened one, all that exists is nothing but the self.

Kena Upanishad: It is derived from its name "*kena*" meaning "by whom". This is the truth of Brahman (the Absolute or God) in relation to nature and man – whether it is the flash of lightening or the wink of the eyes or the thinking of the mind that is shown in the power of Brahman. For this reason, a man should mediate upon Brahman all the time. The reality that strikes man as the power behind everything must be transformed into a permanent realisation. It concludes that austerity, restraint and work are the foundation of the mystical doctrine.

Kathakopanishad: This Upanishad is also called Katha Upanishad. This Upanishad (from the Rig veda) uses a story (*Katha*) involving a young Brahmin to reveal the truth of this world. A father gives his son (Nachiketas) to death (yama) when his son was sacrificing all his possessions, faith entered in him who asked his father to whom he would give him. The father told him that he would give him to death (yama); when the son arrived at the house of death, Yama was not there. He returned after three days and granted him three gifts – (1) his father would cheer him when he returned, (2) he be taught about the sacrificial fire, and (3) the mystery of death would be explained to him. Death tried to make him ask for something else, such as wealth or long life with many pleasures but the son wanted knowledge and not the ignorance. Then the death explained to him how truth is hard to see, but one must enter into the hidden, secret place in the depth of the heart. By considering this as God, one through yoga leaves joy and sorrow behind. The wise reaches their goal and are not born again. It concludes that with the knowledge learned from death, the son attained Brahman and became free from poison and death.

The Prashna Upanishad: Prashna Upanishad means question and this Upanishad is a part of Arthaveda and has six sections dealing with six questions which were asked by six rishis and answered by sage Pippalada –

(1) The root cause of the universe – the creator (*prajapati*).
(2) How many angels support and illumine a creative and which is Supreme – space, air, fire, water, earth, speed, mind, sight and hearing? But the life breath (*prana*) is Supreme.
(3) The relationship between this life – breath and the soul – the life is born from the soul (*atman*).
(4) Concerns sleep, waking and dreams – during sleep, the mind re-experiences what it has seen and heard, felt or thought and known. When one is overcome by light, the God dreams no longer, then all the dreams return to the soul in happiness.
(5) The result of meditating the word *Aum* – meditating on all three letters, the Supreme may be attained.
(6) The spirit with Sixteen parts – the sixteen parts of the spirit are life, faith, space, air, light, water, earth, senses, wind, food, virility, discipline, affirmations, action, world and individuality. All the parts are like spokes of a wheel, the hub of which is the spirit.

Mundaka Upanishad: This Upanishad is associated with the Atharva-Veda. It has two categories, viz. self-realisation and the knowledge of the rational world. Another feature of this Upanishad is the renouncement of all actions, thus encourages the opinion that monkhood is a good way of attaining self-realisation. It also tells the way in which the self-realised souls enter Supreme reality of Brahman and their state afterwards. The Upanishad declares Brahman the first of the gods, the creator of all and the protector of the world.

Mandukya Upanishad: It is associated with Atharva-Veda. This Upanishad explains about – *Aum – Om* – the sacred – and chant the silence at its cessation. Thus, the sacred chant may be used to experience the soul itself. It delineates four levels of consciousness, waking, dreaming, deep sleep which alone will lead one to the path of enlightenment.

Aitareya Upanishad: This Upanishad is associated with Rig-veda. Its deals with *Atman* (the inner self), creation of the universe, qualities of the self or *Brahman*.

Shvetashvatara Upanishad: This Upanishad is a part of Yajur Veda. The questions which are discussed in this Upanishad are – who is God (*Brahman*) who takes care of the universe, who looks after us, and what are the reasons for happiness and sorrow. Besides, the methods of discipline and meditation are recommended to realise the soul by controlling the mind and thoughts. Breathing techniques are also mentioned, as is yoga.

Chandogya Upanishad: This Upanishad belongs to Sama Veda. It deals with sacrifices, forms of worships and also indicate the Vedantic philosophy. It emphasise the importance of chanting the word "*Aum*", which is associated with the life breath (*Prana*). The religious life recommended by this Upanishad has three parts, viz. – (1) sacrifice, study of Vedas giving alms, (2) austerity, and (3) studying the sacred knowledge with the Guru.

Brihadaranyaka Upanishad: This Upanishad is a part of Yajur-Veda. It has three sections, viz. (1) Madhu Khand explains the teachings of the basic identity of the individual and *Atman,* (2) Muni Khand deals with the conversation between the sage Yajnavalkya and his wife Maitreyi, i.e. lead us from the unreal to the real; from the darkness to light and from death to immortality, and (3) Khila Khand – deals with various methods of worship and meditation.

Taittiriya Upanishad: It is a part of Yajur-veda. It is divided into three sections, viz. – (1) Shiksha Valli which deals with the discipline of *Shiksha,* i.e. the study of phonetics and pronunciation (2) Brahmanada Valli – the one who knows Brahman attains Supreme state, and (3) Bhrigu Valli – which describes how the son of Varuna obtained realisation of *Brahman* through repeated takes under his father's guidance.

This Upanishad emphasises "*AUM*", prayers often end with "*AUM*". The goal is to know *Brahman*.

❑

SMRITI

4
Smriti

Smriti literally means 'memory' or that which is remembered. The literature which comprises Smriti was composed after the vedas. It portrays the tradition of the rules on *dharma*, specially those of lawful virtuous persons. It consists of the memories of the wisdom that sages passed on to their disciples and it is their memories that make up the sacred *dharma* and consequently have been recorded to become a written source.

Vedas are the basic religious scriptures upon which the tradition of Indian theism is based. The vedic sages for the benediction of human beings condensed this vast expansion of learning into cryptic form. Their pupils who were of sharp intellect memorised them as soon as these words of great knowledge were pronounced by them (sages).

The main aim of the smriti was to give instructions to the human beings about the behaviour, conduct and administration/supervision, i.e. experienced saints had given the practical and theoretical knowledge of vedas in the smritis which may be divided into three parts – (1) behaviour, (2) conduct, and (3) administration supervision.

Behaviour – development of spiritual life is only possible when one has good behaviour and follows rules and regulations.

Conduct – when the human being lives in a society, he has

to come in contact with other persons everyday in connection with his business, etc. and he gives importance to his selfish deeds leaving behind what is correct or incorrect, which leads to differences and quarrels.

Administration/Supervision – in order to maintain law, order, peace and prosperity, the king used to appoint panchayats and other officials to look after and give punishment to those who used to commit offence. Those who commit wrong doings, their soul pinches them in the long run and finally their life will spiritually lag behind. Like puranas, there are eighteen important Smriti, the details of which are as follows:

Manu Smriti: It deals primarily with matters of the king, state and judicial procedure. It is also known as *ManavaDharmaSastra.* It is written in Sanskrit by Manu who is considred to be the forefather of the mankind, which pertains to the laws of society, family, individual and the nation. It covers subjects like child education, marriage, caste system, status of women in society, etc.

Yagyaval·Kya Samriti: It gives details about the four *ashramas* of life and their respective duties, peace at home, duties of the king and also the important duties of the courts.

Atri Smriti: It gives details of the religious rites and donations to the right person.

Vishnu Smriti: It gives details about the social and religious duties. It also gives importance to family life.

Hareet Smriti: It highlights the Vedic teachings – the four *varnas* and stages, analysis of the Vedas, duties while practicing celibacy, the life and duties of the householder and one who goes to the forest for realisation and the concept of renunciation and of yoga. It also explains the duties of the Brahmin who should have the knowledge of the Vedas and

Smriti – the policies delineated by the Vedas.

Ushanaa Smriti: It gives importance to discipline and also instructions to the *brahmachari* to behave properly wih his guru and all the people.

Katyayan Smriti: It discusses the religious doctrines – the method of performing *havana* and other rituals related to religious activities, pacifying deceased ancestors, description of *trividha kriya* and other rituals.

Vrihaspati Smriti: This smriti gives importance to land donations according to Devaraja Indra and Guru Vrihaspati. As per the views of Vrihaspati, land donations give fruits to gold, silver, clothes, stones, all valuables because everything is got from the land.

Vyas Smriti: It describes the *Grayasthaya Dharma/* family life because man is not complete unless he gets his life partner. Since half man cannot perform all the religious duties, therefore, in order to make himself a complete man, he has to marry. The role of the wife is very important in family life as she looks after the house.

Daksha Smriti: It gives importance to *Ashram Dharma*. Since sage Daksha has given importance to his wife, therefore, the Smriti has given details about the importance of a wife who is obedient and understands the mind of the man by herself. It throws light on *Varnashrama* system which was based on caste and discusses all spheres of human life.

Gautam Smriti: In this smriti, Gautam Muni described the right conduct, celibacy, duties of householder, king, occupation of different castes, duties during times of distress, etc. It also consists of the duties of a person in every stage of life which are according to his caste and social status. There are also ways in which a person can prevent his sins and also its compensation.

Vasishta Smriti: It describes the duties of *Vaishiya* – the one who trades. If the *Vaishiya* wants to store material and sells the same during it's deficiency and then collects wealth, that person (according to this Smriti) is a sinner and dangerous to the society.

Sankha Smriti: This smriti deals with the *Grihasthashram*, to welcome the guests, importance of salvation and the means to attain it. It also gives knowledge about religious ceremonies and rituals, method of chanting the Gayatri mantra, the duties of Brahmin and the different rites and ceremonies connected with the Brahmins.

Apastamba Smriti: The smriti deals with the loss of cow, Brahmin and child due to negligence. It also explains that a person who is following the *Grasthashram*, should also have his duties towards the upkeep of the cows in his home and the work relating to agriculture, etc.

Shatatapa Smriti: The smriti deals from the beginning till the end about the repentance for the elimination of sins. If a person committed a sin in his previous life, he has to face its results in his existing life in the form of distress or any kind of illness, etc.

Samvarta Smriti: The smriti donates the importance of donation in the form of land, money, grains, clothes, etc. but also of wood in order to make fire. It also deals with celibacy, marriage of daughers, repentance for elimination of sins and the importance of Gayatri Mantra.

Likhit Smriti: It discusses *Pind dan* and *Jal dan*. It also describes the sixteen *shradhyas* and the rules and regulations in connection with giving food during *shradhya*.

Yogiras Smriti: It deals in detail with the repentance for elimination of sin, killing of cow and eating of food from the lower caste.

❑

BHAGAWAD GITA

5
Bhagawad Gita

The Yoga of Despondency of Arjuna

King Dhritarashtra was blind by birth. When both the armies of Kauravas and Pandavas gathered at the battlefield of Kurukshetra where the Mahabharata war was fought; Ved Vyas, the author of Gita and Mahabharata and the son of Parasar and Satyavati, gifted Sanjaya the spiritual eye to report the live account of Mahabharata war to king Dhritarashtra.

Ved Vyas gifting Sanjaya the spiritual eye to report the live account of Mahabharata War to Dhitarashtra

The armies of Kaurava and Pandavas were standing and facing each other. The Kaurava army consisted of Dronacharya (guru of both Pandavas and Kauravas),

Kripacharya (Brahmin guru of Hastinapur), Bhishma (son of Santanu and Ganga), Duryodhana (eldest son of Dhritarashtra and Gandari), Karna (son of Surya and Kunti), Ashwathama (son of Dronacharya), Dushashan (younger brother of Duryodhana), Jayadritha (king of Sindhu and son-in-law of Dhrithrashtra), etc. The army of Pandavas had been marshalled so artfully that despite being small it looked big and ferocious. It consisted of the five Pandava brothers (Yudhishthira, Bhima, Arjuna, Nakul and Sahadeva), Drihtadyumna (son of Panchal king Drupad and the brother of Draupadi), Shikhandi (Princess Amba in previous life), Abhimanyu (son of Arjuna and Chitrangda), Drupad (king of Panchal and father of Draupadi), Shalya (grandfather of Nakul and Sahadeva), etc. The sons of Dhritarashtra seemed to be nervous which was generated by the anti-*dharma* bias; on the contrary, the Pandavas stood firm with confidence and courage.

The armies of Kauravas and Panavas facing each other and Lord Krishna positioned his chariot between the two armies on the request of Arjun

When the various sounds of Conch (the Naad) were

heard on earth and the Universe, then Arjuna requested Lord Krishna to position his chariot between the two armies so that he could see his relatives who wanted the war. Accordingly, Lord Krishna positioned the great chariot before Bhishma, Dronacharya and others, in between the two armies. Seeing both the armies, Arjuna spoke to Krishna with a heavy heart seeing in front of him his own relations keen to fight and so positioned, his limbs and various parts of the body were becoming lifeless and his mouth got parched up. His body was shaking and the Gandeeva was slipping from his hand and his skin had the burning sensation all over. He was unfit to even stand and was seeing bad omens. By killing and slaughtering his own kinsman in war, he could not visualise any good to follow at all. He was not keen to get the pleasure and pride of victory in war and the honour of an empire. For whom do we seek kingdom, enjoyment and peace? All those venerable teachers, sons, grandfathers, maternal uncles, brothers-in-law, grandsons and other blood relations had given up their attachment to life and wealth and were in Kurukshetra to fight.

Even if the sons of Dhritarashtra would slay him, he would not wish to slay them in return even for the monarchy of the three *Lokas* (world). By killing all these relatives, they would incur sin. They were blinded by greed and could not see the sin involved in acts of family destruction. Due to deterioration and destruction of family righteousness, the family women loose their morality which gives birth to illegitimate progeny and *vashneya* and those whose family righteousness was destroyed were bound to go to hell. If the armed sons of Dhritarashtra slayed him, that would be more beneficial to him.

After saying these words, Arjuna had put down his bow

and arrows because he thought that it was unfair and sinful to kill his relations for the sake of a kingdom.

Saankhya Yoga

Seeing Arjun in deep distress and his eyes drowned in tears of despondency, Shri Krishna asked him whereupon had that timid anti-heaven honour barring and shameful attachment overcame him at the crisis? He advised him not to succumb to the unmanliness and feeble mindedness which did not suit him, therefore cast off that attachment, stand up to fight. Seeing Arjuna's mind, Lord Krishna was trying to make him wise by pointing out that cowardice did not benefit him and no blemish was more dishonourable for a Kshatriya than fleeing from battle.

Arjuna asked Madhusudan how could he attack Dronacharya or Bhishma who were worth worshipping? By killing them, he would be enjoying the wealth smeared with their blood. His understanding was in chaos and he was completely confused about his duty. Since Arjuna was Lord Krishna's disciple, he seeked his guidance as to what was good for him.

Krishna inducing Arjuna for the battle explaining him the reality

On this Lord Krishna asked Arjuna why was he so worried for those who were not to be worried about. The wisemen mourn neither for the dead nor the alive. As a being, the man experiences in his body the childhood, youth and old age; and after death, the indweller gets a new body, therefore, the wiseman is not disturbed by this phenomenon.

The soul is immortal and eternal and cannot be destroyed. The soul is neither slain nor does it slay. The soul is not born nor dies. As a man casts off his old clothes, similarly, the soul gives up old worn out bodies and puts on new ones. No weapon can pierce this soul. Fire cannot burn it. Neither water can wet it nor wind can dry it. Since death is sure who is born, similarly even birth of the dead is certain, therefore, one should not grieve for the inevitable.

After that, Lord Krishna talked about *Nishkaam Karma* and advised Arjuna to perform his duty and not to desire the results or fruits thereof since he was not the creator of the fruits of his action. Be detached and evenminded both in success and failure. Equanimity of mind is the true state of yoga. Dynamic detachment eliminates the ego and brings proximity to God which is the real aim of yoga. The test of success in yoga is the attainment of equanimity despite success and failure on this ruthless stage of practical action in everyday life. The condition of those who work with desire for fruit of action is miserable. The wise and knowledgeable, by abandoning action that produces results, free themselves from the life and death cycle and attain *Moksha* salvation.

Lord Krishna further told Arjuna that the one who is unattached by all objects and worldly experiences, no ill will attract him and he is free from anger and fear. Such a person is called a Muni. Such egoless person attains peace and *Nirvana*.

Karma Yoga

The theme of this chapter is the performance of duty

with devotion, i.e. *Nishkaam Karma* and doing of duty as *yagya*.

Detached work is the secret of success in this world and also of salvation. God also holds responsible the great people of the world to work selflessly to inspire others. Work is worshipped in this chapter which means duty to be performed with a sense of sacrifice. In chapter second of *Bhagwat Gita*, Lord Krishna explained both Gyan Yoga and *Karma Yoga* and told Arjuna that war was a great opportunity for Kshatriya but at the same time he also explained to Arjuna the merits and usefulness of *Gyan Yoga* for *Moksha*. Arjuna's mind, therefore, got confused. He needed clear instructions from Krishna as to which was the better course of action for him to adopt so that his ambition to attain *Moksha* would be fulfilled.

Lord Krishna explained to Arjuna that the two paths viz *Gyan Yoga* and *Karma Yoga* are not mutually exclusive but are totally apart. There are broadly two types of people – action based and knowledge based. Since the goal of life is salvation which leads to *chitta shuddi* – purity of heart and this purity of heart could be attained both through *Gyan Yoga* – knowledge and *Nishkaam Karma Yoga* – by selfless-action. A man could not attain the state of *Sanyaasa* actionlessness without performing action and by merely withdrawing from action also none can attain perfection.

The true goal of life is *Nirvana* and the path attains the same is through *Gyan Yoga,* i.e. knowledge and *Karma Yoga* i.e., *Nishkaam Karma* which could be attained by action and without *chitta shuddhi,* i.e. conquest of desire one could not accomplish *Karma Yoga* or *Nishkaam Karma*, therefore, perform all good actions and duties without any attachment because one attains the Supreme by performing detached actions. So it is one's duty to perform action keeping in mind the need to inspire people for right action. Whatever conduct and action the elite do, common people follow that. The good people should induce and inspire others by performing their spiritual duty with dedication in a relentless manner. All the actions are performed by three gunas of nature but due to ego, man thinks himself to be the doer. The above three *gunas* are – (1) the *sato guna* binds to the attachment of knowledge and brightness, (2) the *rago guna* to success and fame, and (3) the *tamo guna* binds to ignorance and hypocrisy. The effects of good and bad actions always radiate in all directions, people absorb them according to their level of awakening and knowledge. In view of the above, Lord Krishna advised Arjuna to surrender all his actions to Him and get ready for the war. All sense got attracted by favourable objects and were averse to unfavourable objects. So it is best to avoid their influence since they were the real enemies of the being. (Being a prognative, Arjuna wanted to know the cause of sin and who compels to commit the sin. On this Lord Krishna explained to Arjuna that desire/lust and anger sprout from *rago guna* which compels man to commit sin, therefore, by restraining and controlling the sense, one controls desire. because that sinful lust would be the destroyer of knowledge and realization.) The senses could be controlled through (1) gyan taught by guru and shastras and (2) *Vigyan* acquired through practice. Lord Krishna advised Arjuna to slay the enemy of desire/lust, so that an individual could become victorious, his actions performed for the good of others and become a selfless servant of people and God.

Gyan Yoga – Sanyaas Yoga

In this chapter, Lord Krishna explained to Arjuna how *Nishkaam Karm yoga* is attained to gain the Supreme truth. Battle of life could be won by courage, firm belief in goal and performance of duty with devotion leads to God.

Gyan relating to both God and the soul leads to *Moksha*. Such *gyan* is the fruit of *Karma yoga*. Lord Krishna explained to Arjuna, being his friend and devotee, the same ancient yoga which is the Supreme mystery and knowledge and has been told by Him to Arjuna. Scriptures mention that yoga *vidya,* i.e. God's knowledge is the secret of all secrets, most difficult to comprehend and realise and is beyond mind, imagination, service and intellect; to master this, one has to search for a guru who would guide him. Krishna told Arjuna that this yoga was first explained to Surya, Surya delivered to his son Manu and Manu delivered to his son Ikshwaku. This yoga was known to royal sages but due to long lapse of time, this yoga had vanished.

Upon hearing that, Arjuna asked Lord Krishna that since Surya was born earlier and He was born later, how could he believe that He told the yoga to the Surya – in the beginning. Then Krishna explained to Arjuna that both of them had had many births. He knew them but Arjuna did not. Being the master of the Prakriti/Maaya, He takes birth as and when and the way in which He wanted to appear. To protect the pure, to destroy the wicked and to establish *Dharma*, Lord took birth after ages. Oh Arjuna! he who understood the secret of His divine birth and action correctly, he who asked to come to Him and did not take a new birth.

Sages called them wise whose actions were without motive, desire for results and whose actions were purified by the fire of knowledge. Being detached to the fruit of actions, always contended, such people did not plan with desire and design. Such persons who had abandoned all possessions with controlled mind, needing nothing and merely working with the body incurred no sins. Oh Arjuna! As fierce blaze reduces piles of woods to ashes, similarly, knowledge also burns bad *karmas* to ashes. He who has succeeded in surrendering the fruit of his action to God and destroyed all his doubts through knowledge, such knower of the self was not bound by actions, therefore, Arjun! Rise, stand and fight by cutting off the knot of doubt by the sword of knowledge.

Karma – Sanyaasa Yoga

Lord Krishna told Arjuna that through *Yogasiddhi* or *Nishkaam Karma Yoga* or *Gyan Yoga*, one who has succeeded in surrendering the fruit of his action to God and through knowledge and who has destroyed all his doubts such yogi is now worldly bound.

On hearing this, Arjuna asked Krishna since he is advocating both actions, viz. renunciation as well as performance of action, he wants to know which of the two is better. Upon this, Krishna tells Arjuna that out of the two actions, performance of action is better than the renunciation of action. He thinks *Karma Yoga* is better because it is more effective in attaining full detachment and equanimity, without which neither *Gyan* nor *Smadhi* is possible. In fact, *Karma Yoga* or *Nishkaam Karma* means to work for the good of others, it also means to work for God with devotion. An enlightened man even seeing, hearing, touching, smelling, breathing, talking, discharging body waste, opening and closing eyes, knows that sense and their objects interact independently and he is doing nothing. The *Karmayogi* overcoming attachment performs work with the body, sense, mind and intellect to purify his own self. Further Krishna explains that he who performs actions in a detached manner, surrendering all results of his action to God, remains unaffected by the action results like a lotus leaf in water. A common man binds himself to bondage owing to his attachment to rewards of action but a yogi attains the inner peace by detaching himself from the results of actions. God is neutral and irresponsive to people's good and bad actions, He does not take part in any action either as doer or getting things done, be it good or bad. God has granted free will to all, therefore, people are themselves responsible. One who is detached and not delighted to receive the pleasant and not unhappy to receive the unpleasant and whose self is detached from the external world, will find bliss in the self. By meditating on the Brahman entering the *Samadhi*, he enjoys the permanent, never ending bliss. He who is happy in the self, self-accomplished and self-illumined, that is yogi and by attaining Brahman state gets *Moksha*. Who being internally unaffected by the external worldly objects, by controlling the senses, mind and the intellect, free from desire, anger and fear, pursuing the solitary goal of liberation, such a person is liberated in this world itself. Knowing God as the Supreme Power, who receives all *Yajnas* and looks after the welfare of each being is liked by God.

Atma Sanmyam Yoga

Krishna said – he who performs action without thinking of its result and as a duty, he is true *sanyasi* or yogi. *Sanyaasis* are *tyaagis* because they desire nothing and yogis are *karmis*. The *karma* performed by a yogi is *Nishkaam Karma*, which leads to true *Sanyaasa*. The yoga is the same thing as *Sanyaasa,* i.e. renunciation because nobody can become a yogi without renouncing motive and desire. For a yogi, *Nishkaam Karma* is the most useful way to become an accomplished master. But as he advances in his *Saddhna*, there is always a chance for the worldly allurements to grip his mind. It is, therefore, recommended by shastras that the *karmayogi* should strictly adhere to total inner detachment from the worldly things through *Samadhi*. After going through this, an accomplished yogi is an illumined master, no action can bind him.

Through the use of self, i.e. soul, the self, viz. ego based person should be saved from patan, i.e. debasement because self is both the enemy as well as the friend of the self. He who has succeeded in conquering his lower self-ego, with the higher self, i.e. soul in his own friend but who has not uplifted the lower self, he is his own enemy; hot and cold, pain and pleasure, honour and dishonour do not affect a man with a disciplined self. He who has controlled his mind, intellect and sense fully with knowledge and realisation, such a person is an accomplished yogi. For him, there is no difference between earth, stone and gold. He treats equally his friends, companions, enemies, rivals, opponents, relatives, sinners, etc., such a yogi living alone, disassociating from people, disciplining his body and mind, becomes desireless of possession, free from greed and concentrates his mind on God. The yogi tries to attain the purification of the self by controlling his heart and sense action. By keeping the mind disciplined and concentrating on soul, the yogi attains *Moksha,* i.e. the permanent peace. As a lamp does not flicker in a windless place so is the mind of a yogi which is undistracted by the vagaries of the world. Oh Arjun! That yogi is the supreme who treats and feels the pain and pleasure of others like his own pain and pleasure.

On hearing about a yogi, Arjuna asked Lord Krishna that since the mind is very restless and strong, he finds it hard to control it like a wind. Upon this Lord Krishna advises Arjuna that no doubt the mind is very restless and uncontrollable, but still it can be controlled through practice and renunciation. Arjuna again asked Krishna what happens to a person who has started yoga but who has not controlled his mind? On hearing this Lord Krishna clears Arjuna's doubts by saying Oh Partha! There is no destruction of such a man either in this world or in the next because nobody who performs good acts ever meets bad consequences. Such a yogi after death goes to higher regions where good souls abode and later after coming to earth takes birth in the house of prosperous and devotional people or in the family of a wise yogi. In that family, he develops his own *Sanskaaras* and again works harder to attain the *Siddhi*. Due to his previous *Sanskaaras*, he is attracted to the intutive yoga path and in due course he excels. A yogi man is better than a *Tapaswi,* i.e. ascetic, man of knowledge and even better than ritualists. Therefore, Arjuna! You better become a yogi.

Gyan Vigyan Yoga

Lord Krishna explains to Arjuna that among thousands, hardly one person endeavours to be a *siddha purusha,* i.e. God-realised soul and amongst these ardent seeker harldy one succeeds to know Him truly. Earth, Water, Fire, Air, Ether, Mind, Intelligence and Ego are his eight lower Prakriti i.e., nature but his higher *Prakriti* is, *Chaitanya Shakti*, i.e. the life element upholding the Universe. All being are born out of these two forms of Prakriti. He is the cause of birth, origin and destruction of Universe. He is the fluidity in water, the shine in the moon and the sun, the vedas, Om and sound of the space. He is also the pure fragrance in earth, the energy in fire, the life element in all living beings and devotion in all ascetics. He is that great power of the strong which is devoid of lust and attachment. The three desires *Satvik* (good), *Rajsik* (practice) and *Tamsik* (negative) are the components of *Prakriti*. People attached to and deluded by the above three *gunas* of *Prakriti*, do not know Him. The *illusion,* i.e. *Maaya* created by Him is made up of the above three *gunas* which is His creation and is therefore, very hard to suppress, only His devotees surmount it.

Further Krishna tells Arjuna that the enlightened devotee is great since he is devoted, therefore, dear to Him. No doubt, all the great but the *Gyani*, the spiritually enlightened is firmly established in Him. After many births, the enlightened man takes refuge in Him and realises that He alone is God, such kind of people are rare. The deluded people whose intellect is confused by different desires and pray to other gods with devotion and perform different rites, He fortifies his faith in devotional pursuits. The aforesaid people who worship the deity with devotion as chosen by them, they get the results and He is the giver of such rewards to them. The results of prayers that are obtained by the man of limited intellect are short lived. The worshipper of gods and deities go to them but His worshippers come to Him. People lacking in wisdom are unaware of His supreme reality. Since He is covered by His *yoga Maaya*, therefore, is birthless and even changeless. The people under the cover of *Maaya* cannot know God but only devotees who have mastered yoga can pierce the veil of *Maaya* and see God.

Shri Krishna explains to Arjuna that He knows all beings in the past, present and future but none knows Him due to the lack of spiritual knowledge. The performers of good deeds, whose sins have ended due to their devotion, they worship Him with devotion and determination and such people for the sake of getting rid of the snare of age and death, realise the *Param Brahman* and know all secrets of *Karma*, even remember Him at the hour of death.

Rajvidhyarajguah Yoga

The yoga of Supreme Knowledge and Mystery

Shri Krishna is supreme and respectable. He has a great bondage with the human beings through *bhakti*. A person who has sowed the seeds of His *bhakti* in his heart, he will definitely reach out to Him. Lord Krishna told Arjuna that he had not envied Him and followed Him, therefore, He will tell him the supreme mystery of God knowledge (*gyan*) and God realization (*vigyan*). With that knowledge and realization, he would be free forever from this world and attain *Moksha*. Krishna calls the knowledge of God Realization Supreme and highly secret as it relates to the transcendental nature of Brahman. It is directly realizable through yoga and easy to practice when followed in accordance with *Dharma*. Those men who does not have *Shraddha* or faith in *Dharma*, they return to the world after death taking rebirth and does not attain Him.

Lord Krishna further tells Arjuna that the entire Universe is in Him in the un-manifested form. All beings are in Him. He created the multitude of beings time after time, who are helpless under the power of His *Maaya*. Ignorant people do not know His higher nature therefore, disregard His presence in all human forms. People of irrational desires, thoughtless actions, possessing useless knowledge and having egoistic and *Rajsik* nature take refuge in destructive *Prakriti*. Such people could not realize the transcendental and cosmic reality of the Divine, people of *Tamsik* nature are more ignorant and foolish and are sunk deeper into the sea of ignorance. But the people of Divine nature worship Him with devoted mind. Such people worship Him in different ways like *Bhajan-Kirtan* and some by devotionally prostrating before Him. Lord Krishna further told Arjuna that He is yogya, Swadha, Mantra, Fire, Ghee, Homa, Herb and is the provider and giver of the fruit of action. He is the sole knewable power and Om. Besides he is all the four Vedas, viz. Rig, Yajun, Atharva and Saam Veda.

Lord Krishna further tells Arjuna that He is the parent of this world and also the grandfather, the provider and giver of the fruit of action. He creates heat, attract water and thus causes rains. He is deathless and death, visible and the invisible being. The worshippers of Devas go to Devas, Pitras to Pitras, Bhootas to Bhootal but His devotees come to Him only. Who worships Him with devotion by offering leaf, flower, fruit and water, He accepts such offerings made with intense love. Oh Kaunteya! By surrendering your good and bad actions to Him, by fixing your mind on Him and making him the only God of your life, you would come to Him.

Vevhuti Yoga

Lord Krishna tells Arjuna, since he is His friend, he would explain to him which had not been told earlier for his benefit, the highest Supreme knowledge – the *Brahma Gyan*.

Persons who know Him as birthless, beginning less and the Supreme Lord, such persons are above delusion, sinless and attain to His intelligence, knowledge, poise, forgiveness, truth, control of action sense, control of knowledge senses, pleasure, pain, birth, death, fear, bravery, non-violence, equanimity, contentment, alms giving and fame. (defame these qualities of people emanate from Him) he who understands His supreme yoga and divine manifestation his life energy concentrates on Him would always be in peace and contentment. On hearing this, Arjuna asked Lord Krishna since He is the *Param Brahma* – the Supreme purity, the eternal divinity, birthless and omnipresent still he wants to know the powers by which He pervades the world which only He can describe.

On hearing Arjuna, Lord Krishna explained that He is the soul seated of all beings and the cause of birth, continuity and death of all beings, of the vedas He is the Saama Veda, of the Devas He is the Indra, of the senses He is the mind and of the beings He is the consciousness, among the Redras, Yakshas and Vassur, He is Shankar, Kubera and fire respectively.

He is also Meru, Brihaspati. He is also the Om, Kaam-adhenu, Vasuki, Shesha Naga, Varuna, lion, Garuda and Ganga, in the cows, serpents, nagas, water, life, animals, birds and rivers respectively. He is also the beginning, the middle and the end of all beings that are born, Marghashirsha in months, spring among the seasons when the flowers blossom, punishing power of the punishers, the silence of the secret and wisdom of the wise. He is also the cause of the birth and origin of all the beings since His divine manifestations are endless, He has exposed a gist of the same to him. All grandeur, power, prosperity, gorgeousness that he sees, reflect His radiance. He supports and sustains the Universe with a fragment of Him.

Vishwaroopa Darshan Yoga

Arjuna showed his desire to see Lord Krishna's infinite form which is the cause of creation, maintenance and dissolution of all the beings. Then Lord Krishna gives Arjuna the divine eyes in order to watch His divine yoga or forms. Arjuna saw countless mouths, arms and astonished scenes in the *Vishwaroopa* of God. The divine form is draped with heavenly attaire of full shine and glitter, celestial garlands exuding aromas, oranments with amazing shine and countless faces shining all over. The shine of *Vishwaroopa* is beyond the enormous shine of the light of a thousand suns blazing all at once. Arjuna is amazed to see the aforesaid form. Arjuna sees all Devtas/ gods, like Brahma, Vishnu and Mahesh, hosts of divine Rishis, all serpents. He also sees Him with numerous arms, stomachs, with celestial eyes, bodies covering space on all sides. He sees gods everywhere, in all directions and yet His beginning, middle or the end were vastly beyond his vision. He saw Him supporting *Mukut* (crown), *Gada* (Mace), *Chakra* (discus) with radiance of blinding shine everywhere, glaring lights, blazing forth like fierce fires and suns and in all directions. Arjuna is afflicted with fear after seeing this infinite form touching the sky, sparkling with countless colours, massive mouth opens aghast, massive fiery eyes. Arjuna further tells Him that he saw all the sons of Dhritarashtra, their chiefs and many kings were rushing into His frightening mouth. In that all devouring form, he asked him to tell him who is he? Then Lord Krishna tells Arjuna that He is the mighty death, power of the time force, the destroyer of all people.

Irrespective of Pandavas, all those fighting in the army of Kaurvas would die, therefore, tells Arjuna to stand up and fight. By winning the victory he would become famous and enjoy the Rajya. They already had been killed by Him, and he is just a mere agent.

On hearing Lord Krishna's words, Arjuna tells him with folded hands that it is naturally right that the world feels deeply rejoiced in His devotional praise; He is the only Supreme power to be worshipped. Arjuna bowed down and requested Him to forgive him, just like a friend forgives his friend, father to his son and a husband to his beloved. Again Arjuna requested Krishna to show Him the same previous *Vishwaroopa* or *Chaturbhuja* form.

Lord Krishna tells Arjuna that He showed His *Vishwaroopa* to him out of love and grace, nobody had seen His this form earlier. Neither the study of vedas, nor performance of *yagya*, nor giving alms, rituals, penance and austerity could enable anyone to see His *Vishwaroopa*. O Arjuna! One who is devoted, considering Him the Supreme source, loves to everyone attains Him.

Bhakti Yoga

The easiest way to get Lord Krishna's love is through Bhakti Yoga.

Arjuna asked Lord Krishna which devotee is a greater yogi, viz. who worships Him with total attachment and devotion or he who worships the *Nirguna* or *Param Brahma*? Lord Krishna replied that those who worship Him with full devotion and mind are perfect. But those who worship the omnipresent, *Sachinanda Brahma* by controlling their senses, by exercising the equanimity of mind and committing the welfare of all beings also come to Him – this form (*Nirguna*) of worship and devotion is very difficult because it needs effective control of the senses and purification of mind, which means that the world of senses is unreal and only Brahma or soul is real. But those who surrender and renounce all actions to Him and worship Him with devotion, regard Him as the highest goal and concentrate on Him alone and perform all actions for His sake, will attain Him. Lord Krishna asked Arjuna if he is unable to fix his mind on Him, then endeavour to seek Him through Abhyas Yoga, incase he is unable to practice this yagya then concentrate on performing all actions for His sake, by this he can attain Him. Even if he is unable to do this, he can take full refuge in Him while controlling his senses.

Further He said that he who has no envy for anyone, is kind hearted, detached, egoless, evenminded in pain and pleasure, contended and firmly fixing devotee is dear to Him. By whom nobody gets injured and who does not get injured by others, and is free from pleasure, jealousy, fear, anger and worry is dear to Him. Also he who has no desire for sense objects, internally pure, no friend or foe, not a hypocrite, unoffended by the unwelcome, above grief and longing, indifferent to vice or virtue, unaffected by hot and cold, pain and pleasure, praise and criticism, silent, contended, firm of mind and devotion is dear to Him. Those who follow Him with faith and devotion are intensely dear to Him.

Kshetra – Kshetragya Yoga

Lord Krishna tells Arjuna that the body is called *Kshetra* – the field of action likewise the power that knows this field is called *Kshetragya* – soul by the wise. The true knowledge is the knowledge of the *Kshetra* and *Kshetragya* which have been explained by the rishis in many ways. Five Bhoota (elements – earth, air, water, fire and sky) ego, intelligence, *mool prakriti*, mind, ten senses (five knowledge and five action), five senses of Indriya (*Sabdth, Sprash, Roop, Rus, Gandth*), desire, repulsion, pain, pleasure, *chetna* – aggregate of body forces, consciousness and firmness are the *Kshetra*. Humility, no hypocrisy, non-violence, forgivenss, simplicity, service to Guru, purity, steadfastness, self-control, detachment from sense objects of attraction, absence of egoism, to have the right appreciation of the pain during the birth, death, old age and sickness, mental detachment, continued faith in soul, knowledge and intuitive meditation and understanding of the *tatva gyan,* i.e. the real truth, are the means to *Gyan* – knowledge/God and what contradicts is ignorance.

Lord Krishna tells Arjuna that he would tell him it is only God who must be known. After knowing God the knower attains the *Param Brahma*. The external world can be known with the mind and the senses but the internal reality can be seen only with spiritual discipline. Being undivided in all beings yet He appears divided in them. Being the creator, supporter and destroyer (Brahma, Vishnu and Mahesh). He is the source of all light even of the Sun, no darkness touches Him. The only means to know Him is through *Braham Vidya*, which is a secret knowledge and guru can impart it. People see God through meditation, through Guru, knowledge through meditation *Dhyana Yoga* can see God in his own self and *Karma Yoga* - working selflessly for others and God. Besides, people not knowing the above three ways of worship, pray to Him as they hear from others and due to their devotion and dedication, they also go beyond death. As the sun lights up the whole world, similarly the soul illumines the whole *Kshetra* body. The

Kshetra is this body but a person is unaware of the inner soul - the soul which illumines the body but when he sees the inner light, his darkness will disappear and the dawn of bliss will descend on him. Those who with the eye of knowledge successfully discern the distinction between *Kshetra* and *Kshetragya* and know the way of freeing from action, attain the Supreme God.

Gunastriyavibagh Yoga

Lord Krishna tells Arjuna that he would tell him that Supreme knowledge by knowing which all the munis/ great ones have attained *Mukti* and realised the Supreme. By mastering knowledge, they attained Him, neither aggrieved at the time of *pralaya* or of new creation, they are born again. The *Prakriti* is his womb into which He places the life seed, from which all beings are born.

In all wombs, whatever bodies are being produced, *Prakriti* is their mother womb and He is the father providing the seed. The three *Gunas* of *Prakriti,* viz. *Sattva*, *Rajas* and *Tamas,* viz. purity, desire and inertia are the eternal soul to the body. The *Sattva guna* is pure and stainless and binds the being to good use. The *Rajas guna* is the source of intense device, desire and attachment and it binds the being to action. *Tamo guna* is born out of ignorance and it binds the being to sleep, sloppiness and indulgence.

Sattava guna is in a dominating position. Similarly, the desire to acquire wealth, lack of peace, passion, possession of all assets, greeed, ambition and passion are indication of the prominence of the *Rajas guna* while insensitivity towards duty, sleep, lust, anger are the characteristics of a *Tamsik*. The results of the *Sattvik*, *Rajsik* and *Tamsik* are pure, pain and ignorance respectively. Similarly, all the three gunas, viz. *Sattva*, *Rajas* and *Tamas* give rise to spiritual knowledge, greed and attachment, ignorance respectively. *Sattava guna* people move *Swargyuni* – heaven, *Rajsiks* to the *Manava yuni* – middle and *Tamas* get the lower *loka*. If the being overcomes the above three *gunas* of *Sattva, Rajas* and *Tamas*, he becomes free from birth, age and death and attains *Mukti*. Conquered through his spiritual knowledge Arjuna asked Lord Krishna about the symptoms of the being who has conquered or overcome these three *gunas* of *Prakriti*. Lord Krishna explained to Arjuna that a Gunatel - who has arisen above the mentioned three *gunas* of Prakriti Sattva, Rajas and Tamas is same in pain and pleasure, joy and sorrow, treating stone and gold alike; same in honour and dishonour; friend and foe; unaffected by praise and criticism; not egoistical and who worships Him in faith and devotion by overcoming the three *gunas*, *Satvik, Rajas* and *Tamas* is fit to reach *sachitananda Brahmnas*.

Purushottama Yoga

This world is an imperishable tree, its leaves are the vedas and he who knows this tree is knower of the vedas. The nature of this worldly tree is not known, i.e. its beginning, existence and end is not known. But one can cut this worldly tree with the solid axe of renunciation, after this, one has to look for that source, reaching where one does not come back again. A person who reaches this place – the Brahmn, is free from honour, attachments and sense contact, concerned firmly in soul, desire, rising above pain and pleasure and that is His *Param Dharma* – the Supreme abode from where neither the sun, moon nor the fire illumine.

Further Lord Krishna tells Arjuna that the soul activates the five senses and the mind just like the wind carries the smell from one place to another, similarly the soul enters the body and when it leaves the body, the soul takes with it its mind and senses and takes a new birth. The unwise people do not know this, only the spiritually awakened Yogi can see the same in their bodies through spiritual power. The light which is seen in the sun, moon and fire is all due to this radiance. He supports all beings by entering the earth through His power. He enters the moon and supports the medical herb. (God by entering the earth and moon, by which He supports the basic life forces and becoming the caring face in herbs, helps the beings to treat and cure themselves.) He is seated in the hearts of all beings. He is also the creator of the vedas and the real knower of the vedas; therefore, He is known as *Purushottama* – the Supreme being. O Bharata! The being who knows Him in this manner knows all and he worships Him with full devotion. Lord Krishna tells Arjuna that the Supreme knowledge has been impacted by Him, knowing this, the knowledgeable becomes enlightened.

The Yoga of the Divine

This chapter describes the characteristics of the people of divine orientation and those of demonical nature. The former are sincere devotees who worship out of love to know God without any material or worldly gains, they are fearless, pure by heart, faith in the yoga, knowledgeable, giving alms, have control on their senses, make sacrifices, know the scriptures, simple, non-violent, angerless, speaking the truth, peace loving, compassionate towards all, detached, gentle, humble and firm, forgiving, courageous, pure by heart and lack conceit. The latter, even if they worship, they do it for personal gains and propogation. Such people are hypocrite, conceited, arrogant, have false pride, anger, crudeness, ignorant of the spiritual do's and dont's, lack purity and right conduct, they hold the view that the world is not real, deny moral basis of the world, it is without God, its cause is the male-female union and nothing else. They are the enemies of the world and are born for the destruction of the world. Their main interest is to look after the bodily interests and its maintenance. They distance themselves from the company of the wise and consider the study of scriptures as a waste of time. Such people are destructive for the good in society, in fact, they are the real enemies of peace and progress of the world. They follow unworthy principles and due to greed and ignorance, possess evil ideas, indulge them in collection and possession of material assets for gratification of lust and desires which they believe to be the only goal of life. Such people are slaves to hundreds of carnal desires and ambitions. Their lives being slave to lust and anger, they waste it in amassing wealth through unworthy means. They think that they have killed this enemy, will definitely kill other enemies also. They think themselves to be above all, powerful, happier and enjoyer of all things, will perform *yagya*, distribute gifts deep in the clutches of lust, hell of course is their destination.

Krishna tells Arjuna that such demonical people are the lowest of human beings in this world. Since lust, anger and greed are the three gates to hell and such people indulge themselves in it and therefore, destroy their self (*jeeva*). Further Krishna explains to Arjuna that one should detach himself from those three (lust, anger and greed), the gates of destruction and the person who practices what is spiritually good for him, only he can reach the Supreme state; he who by ignoring the scriptures acts of his own accord and desire cannot achieve perfection, then he loses happiness and also the Supreme state, therefore, scriptures are the best authority to guide on the spiritual do's and dont's and also as to what duty is. After knowing the scriptural injunctions and guidance, we should act accordingly.

The Yoga of Three-fold Faith

Arjuna asks Krishna how is the worship of those reckoned who perform *yagya* and prayers with devotion but not in accordance with the scriptural injunctions. Is that of *Rajsik, Tamsik* or *Satvik* nature. Krishna tells Arjuna that *Shraddha* (devotion to God) of the beings (devotees) is born in their three-fold respective nature, Satvik, Rajsik and *Tamsik*. *Satvik* people worship *Devas*, *Rajsiks* worship *Yakshas* and *Rakshasas* and the *Tamsik* worship *Pretas* and *Bhootas*.

Further Krishna tells Arjuna, just as beings are fond of eating three kinds of foods in accordance with their nature, similarly there are three kinds of *yagyas* (sacrifices), *tapas* (austerities) and *Daanas* (charities). The foods that contribute to longevity, brilliance, vigour, health, juicy, imparting energy and savour are liked by the *Satviks*. The food that is bitter, sour, over-spiced, over-hot, exciting, which generates pain, regret and disease is liked by the *Rajsiks*. The food that is uncooked, cold, stale, tasteless, stinking and of impure quality is liked by the *Tamsiks*. Similarly, the *yagya* performed by people without intentions of reward, with full devotion strictly in accordance with the scriptures is the *Satvik yagya*. The *yagya* which is performed with the intentions of reward and return is called the *Rajsik yagya*. The *yagya* which is not performed in accordance with the scriptural instructions and without *Shraddha*, in which no *Mantras* are recited, no meals are offered and no alms are distributed is the *Tamsik yagya*.

The charity which is offered carefully to such a needy and deserving person who is incapable of offering any return, given at an opportune time and place, with an understanding that it is one's duty to give alms to a worthy person is called a *Satvik* alm. The alm which is given with the hope and intention of return or reward and which is done half heartedly is *Rajsik* alm and the charity which is offered to an undeserving person with arrogance or disrespect at a wrong time and place is called *Tamsik* alms.

Austerity which is performed by devoted and disciplined people with dedication, without any expectation of reward or return is called *Satvik*. Love for God emerges only in pure hearts. Austerity also means creative endeavour, i.e. performing great acts selflessly for the good of all; the austerity performed with the idea of attaining worldly recognition, possession, honour is merely hypocrisy and yields uncertain and momentary rewards is called *Rajsik*; and the austerity performed out of ignorance by inflicting self-torture and with a view to destroying others is called *Tamsik*.

Krishna further explained to Arjuna that *Aum, Tat* and *Sat* are the three names of God (*Brahamn*). The importance of the word *Aum* is so great that while performing the *yagya, daana* or *tapa* (sacrifice, charity and austerity) this pure, pious and spiritually auspicious word is uttered at the beginning. *Aum* is to be realised through spiritual *Saadhana* (guru given technique), *Aum* realisation means seeing and feeling God, in the form of soul, in the body. The ardent seeker of God realization (*Moksha*) perform the actions of *yagya, daana* or *tapa* without any wish for gain or return by concentrating on *Tat* (which means God); we know that butter is inside the milk but without following a particular process, we cannot separate the butter from milk. Similarly, without acting on the guru's advice, we cannot attain *tat*. Similarly, the word '*sat*' is used in respect of the divinity (the ultimate reality) and purity. It is also used in respect of the spiritual well-being. It signifies the ultimate reality, the *Brahamn*.

All religious sacrifices like *havan, yagya, daana* and *tapa* performed without *Shraddha* are called Asat. No benefit accrues from it either in this world or in the next.

The Yoga of Salvation

Arjuna asked Krishna about *Sanyaasa* and *Tyaaga* and the difference between them. Thereupon Krishna explained to him that the wise men know the renunciation of *Kaamya Karma* (desire-based actions) to be *Sanyaasa* and the learned ones call the renunciation of the fruits of all actions as *Tyaaga*. There are three kinds of *Tyaaga – Satvik, Rajsik* and *Tamsik*. *Satvik tyaaga* is that which is observed and performed out of spontaneous love and devotion to God for self-purification. *Rajsik* is that which is observed in the hope of getting better rewards from the *devas* while those who give up performance of duty as relief from struggle are called *Tamsik*.

All dutyful actions performed with a sense of duty, without ego, attachment or desire for results are called *Satvik*. The action which is performed out of sheer attachment, without reason, ignoring one's own capability to accomplish it the quality of results and aimed at causing pain to others is called *Tamsik*. While the action which is performed with a craving out of ego, the feeling that 'I am the doer' is called *Rajsik* action.

Similarly, there are three types of distinctions of intelligence and firmness in accordance with their respective qualities. The intelligence which knows worthy and unworthy paths of the *karma*, right or wrong actions, fear and fearlessness, bondage and salvation is the Satvik intelligence. The intellect that understands incorrectly the ways of *dharma* and *adharma* (righteousness and unrighteousness), the worthy and unworthy action is called *Rajsik*, while the intelligence which sees *dharma* in *adharma* and sees all things in an opposite way is called *Tamsik* intelligence.

There is threefold happiness. The happiness which is acquired through long practice gives deep joy, entails the end of sorrow and is born out of the spiritual cultivation of the intellect is called *Satvik*. The happiness which emanates from the contact of senses with their (respective) objects is called *Rajsik* while the happiness which is full of delusion to one's own self and is born of sleep, sloth and delusion is called *Tamsik* happiness. All *karmas* (duties) of Brahmins, Kshatriyas, Vaishyas and Shudras are assigned according to the merit born out of their nature. *Shama* (forgiveness), austerity, purity, straight forwardness, knowledge, realisation and faith in God are the natural duties of Brahmins. Bravery, vigour, courage, efficicency, not to flee from battlefield, giving alms, generosity and supremacy in administration are the duties of Kshatriyas born of their nature. Agriculture, cattle care and honesty in business are the duties of the Vaishyas. The duty of service to others is born out by shudras.

He who pervades the entire Universe, and the will to work, worship Him with his own duty, attains perfection. One's own *Dharma* (duty) is always better even if it lacks perfection than other's *Dharma*, be it superior. No sin accrues to a person who performs his duty born of his nature (which is in accordance with his intrinsic nature).

In the end, Krishna tells Arjuna that a person on

attaining the *Brahamn* is saturated with spirit, serene minded even in loss and gain, he is the same to all beings and attains to the highest devotion in Him. By His grace, he (Arjun) will overcome all grief and pain, by fixing his mind fully on Him, but if due to egoism, he does not listen to Him, he will destroy himself. On the basis of ego, if he thinks that he will not fight, such a conclusion will be unrealistic because his own nature will force him to fight. With total devotion and surrender to Him, he will achieve Supreme peace and Supreme state.

Krishna further advises him to concentrate his mind on Him, worship Him, be devoted to Him, surrender himself to Him, then he will attain Him, this is His promise to him because he is very dear to Him. Abandoning all *Dharmas*, surrender himself fully to Him. He will free him from all sins. A person who listens to Gita with devotion and faith, is freed from all sins and goes to higher regions deserved by the righteous souls.

Arjuna at last tells Krishna that by His grace, his delusion has been destroyed, he is firm and would act as per His teachings.

Sanjaya after hearing the discourse between Vasudeva and Arjuna tells King Dhritarashtra – on whichever side Yogeshwara Lord Krishna and Arjuna are, there is sure success, victory, power, prosperity and eternal justice.

❑

MAHABHARATA

6
Mahabharata

Ved Vyasa, the compiler of the Vedas, composed the Mahabharata. His parents' names were Satyawati and Parasara. He had an Ashram at Alaknanda near Badrinath, where he wrote the Mahabharata, an epic.

In Mahabharata, there are 18 *Parvas*, i.e. parts. The character of the epic move with the vitality of real life. It portrays on the one side charity, renunciation or *tyaga, typsya, upkar*, truth, good behaviour, love and courage but on the other hand deals with greed, lust, bitterness, selfishness, cruelty, hatred and conspiracies. Undoubtedly, it has the gist of Indian cultured life, warfare, *dharma, karma* and *moksha*.

Aadhi Parva

In ancient India, there was a famous king known as Yayati whose kingdom was Khandavaprastha. He had two queens, namely Devayani and Sarmishtha. Devayani was the daughter of *asura* Sukracharya and Sarmishtha was the daughter of king of *asuras* Vrishaparva. Devayani gave birth to two sons, namely Yadu and Truvarsu and Krishna was born in this Vansha. Sarmishtha gave birth to three sons, the youngest of them was Puru who was made the king by Yayati. The kings were called Puru vanshi after the name of Puru. After some dynasties, Dushyunta became the king of Puru dynasty who married Sakuntala, they had a son named

Bharat and 'Bharata' is the name after him. There came a famous king named Hastin who established the kingdom of Hastinapur. Kuru was the descendent of Hastin whose descendants were called Kauravas and the famous place of Kurukshetra is named after Kuru.

King Santanu married Ganga who gave birth to eight sons and each son she took and immersed in the river. Santanu was filled with horror and anguish at her conduct but suffered it all in silence due to the promise he had made to her. Ganga killed seven children and when the eighth child was born, she was about to throw it into the ganges, Santanu stopped her from killing the child. Ganga told him her story of how Vasishtha cursed her and the eight Vasus to be born in the world of man. She took the eighth child with the promise that she would bring up the child and then return to him as a gift. The child who was given the name of Devavrata was well versed and mastered in the art of arms, archery from Parasurama and learnt the Vedas and Vedanta from sage Vasishtha. One day when Santanu was wandering along the banks of Ganges, he saw a boy casting a dam of arrows across the Ganges and playing in the mighty rivers with an indulgent mother and Santanu was amused at the sight, Ganga came and revealed herself and handed over the child to him and disappeared. Santanu crowned Devavrata as his Yuvaraja, his heir.

One day, king Santanu was wandering on the bank of Yamuna, he saw Satyavati, daughter of a fisherman and showed his desire to marry her. The father agreed with the condition that the son of Satyavati would be the king after him. Since Santanu had already decided Devavrata as his heir, he did not reveal the matter to anyone, therefore, returned to his capital, Hastinapur. When Devarata came to know about his father's desire to marry Satyavati, he vowed with upraised arms to his father that he would never marry and dedicate himself to the life of unbroken chastity and the sons of Satyavati would be the heir of Santanu.

Devavrata pledged for *brahamacharya* and he was known as Bhishma, which means one who undertakes a terrible vow and fulfils it. Satyavati got married to Santanu and two sons were born to them, viz. Chitrangada and Vichitravirya ascended the throne. Chitrangada was killed in a battle. When Vichitravirya attained the marriageable age, the princess of Kasi, namely Amba, Ambika and Ambalika were brought forcefully, later Amba was released and Ambika and Ambalika were married to him. Dhritarashtra and Pandu were born respectively from the two queens. Since Dhritarashtra was blind from birth, Pandu ascended the throne.

At the same time, a son was born to the servant maid of Ambalika, who was named as Vidura. He was regarded as Mahatma who was unparalleled for his knowledge of *dharma, sastras* and statesmanship and was totally devoid of attachment and anger. Bhishma appointed him as the chief counsellor of King Dhritarashtra.

Dhritarashtra got married to Gandhari, the daughter of Gandhar king. Being loyal, she too put cloth on her eyes. One hundred sons and one daughter were born to her. Duryodhana was the eldest son and Dushala was the daughter who was married to Jayadratha of Sindhu.

Pandu got married to Pratha, daughter of king Sursey of Yadvanshi, Yadava race. Since she was brought up or adopted by her cousin Kuntibhoga, she was known as Kunti. Kunti was the Bua of Lord Krishna. When Kunti was young, sage Durvasa was so pleased with her that he gave her a divine *mantra* and by reciting the *mantra* she could call upon any God. Since she wanted to test the power of the boon granted to her by sage Durvasa, she called upon Surya and was blessed with a son who was born with divine armour and earrings and was bright like the sun who was known as Karṇa. (Durvasa granted her this boon because he foresaw by his yogic power the misfortune which was in store for her future.)

Kunti became the unwedded mother, due to fear she placed the child in a sealed box and set it afloat in a river. A childless charioteer happened to see the floating case and was surprised to see a beautiful child. He handed it over to his wife. Thus, Karna; the son of the Sun God, brought up as a charioteer's child was known as *Sutputra*.

When the time came, she got married to king Pandu and had three sons, viz. Yudhishthira, Bhima and Arjun and with the second wife of Pandu, named Madri, two sons were born, namely Nakul and Sahadeva. The sons were born in the forest among ascetics. Pandu lived for years in the forest with his wives and children. Due to the curse of the sage, Pandu died and since Madri felt that she was responsible for the death of Pandu, she burnt herself on the pyre of her husband. Thus, the sages of the forest took grief-stricken Kunti and the Pandavas to Hastinapur and entrusted them to Bhishma. The five sons of Pandu and hundred sons of Dhritarashtra grew up at Hastinapur. As they grew up, Kripacharya taught them archery and the practice of arms and other things.

After the death of Pandu, Duryodhana thought that as his blind father was quite helpless, he must prevent Yudhishthira's accession to the throne. He thought that the powers of the Pandavas would decline with the death of Bhima, therefore, made arrangements to kill him. He went along with his brothers and Pandavas for a swim in the Ganges. He also mixed poison in his food, Bhima felt drowsy and lay down on the bank of the river. The poisonous food he had taken was counteracted by the snake poison and no harm came to Bhima and the river washed him to the bank. Duryodhana thought that Bhima must have died with poisonous snakes and fanged with spikes, he returned with others in great joy to the kingdom. Sometime later, Bhima awoke and came back. Kunti and her sons welcomed him. The poison entered his system and he became stronger than before.

The Pandavas and the Kauravas learnt the practice of arms first from Kripacharya and later from Dronacharya, who was became the master in the art of archery which Parasurama taught him. He married the sister of Kripa and a son Aswathama was born to them. Bhishma decided that

Dronacharya teaching the art of archery to Pandavas and Kauravas

Dronacharya was the fittest person to impart further instructions to the Pandavas and Kauravas. He received him with special honour and employed him to master the princes in the use of arms. Amongst them, Arjuna was the best. Nobody could beat him, that is why Dronahcarya also loved him the most.

One day Dronacharya wanted to examine the princes. He put a sparrow on one of the highest branches of the tree. He first called upon Yudhishthira and asked him what he could see? He said that he saw a sparrow and him. Dronacharya was not happy with his answer, therefore, he called one by one all the princes but was not impressed by their answers. Lastly, he called Arjuna and asked him the same question. He answered that he could only see the eye of the sparrow and he left the arrow on the bow into the eye of the sparrow which speared the eye.

All the Pandavas became very famous for their behaviour in Hastinapur. The people of the city used to praise them openly and declared that Yudhishthira was alone fit to be the king. They also became known of their archery. Duryodhana was worried about becoming the heir and preventing Yudhishthira's chances of accession to the throne. Since Yudhishthira was the eldest amongst Pandavas and Kauravas, therefore, he was considered as their heir apparent. Duryodhana, being the eldest son of Dhritarashtra considered himself to be the heir of the throne.

The jealousy of Duryodhana began to grow at the sight of the physical strength of Bhima and the dexterity of Arjuna. Karna and Sakuni, his mother's brother became his counsellors in his evil plannings. One day, he planned with them to send the Pandavas to Varanavata. He met Purochana (the minister) and gave him instructions to make a beautiful palace made of wax, jute, lac, ghee, oil and fat for the Pandavas reception. The materials used for plastering the walls were also inflammable. He skilfully filled up the various parts of the building with dry things which could catch fire easily. The plan was when the Pandavas had settled down in the wax house, to set it on fire at night when they were sound asleep. However, Vidur came to know about the plan and he sent an expert miner with the instructions to the Pandavas living in the wax house. The miner worked for many days in secret, unknown to the Purochana and completed a subterranean tunnel from the wax house right under and across the walls and the moat which ran around the precincts. The Pandavas and their mother Kunti used to sleep at the end of the tunnel, so that in case fire, they could run out easily.

Yudhishthira came to know about the plans of Purochana. He did his *yagya* that day and served food to the local people. Amongst the people who came, there was a Bhilni who came with her five sons. After having their food, they slept at one corner of the palace. At night, Bhima set fire to the palace in several places and the whole palace was reduced to ashes. In the morning, when the people saw the bodies of Bhilni and her five sons, they thought Kunti and her five sons died in the fire. Dhritarashtra and his sons were happy from inside but they cast off their royal garments in token of mourning for the Pandavas whom they believed were consumed in the fire.

The five Pandavas came out from the wax house and reached the jungle, they saw a boat sent by Vidura in which they crossed the Ganges in darkness. In the forest, Bhima killed Hidim and got married to his sister Hidimba and a son was born out of their wedlock and his name was Ghatotkacha, a very brave warrior. When the Pandavas were ready to leave the forest to go further, Ghatotkacha along with his mother Hidimba went to the Himalayas. While going, he told his father Bhima, whenever there would be any necessity of him, he would come for their rescue.

The Pandavas were living in disguise as brahmins at Ekachakrapra for months when they heard the news of the *Swayamvara* of Draupadi, the daughter of Draupada, king of Panchala. They proceeded with their mother Kunti to Draupada's kingdom in order to witness the *Swayamvara*.

They reached the city and hid themselves in the house of a potter as obscure brahmins of no note. They also came to know that Draupti was born out of fire. Draupada placed a steel bow and the candidates had to string the bow and with it shoot a steel arrow through the central aperture of a revolving disk at a target placed high. Draupada proclaimed that he who would perform that feat, would marry his daughter.

Many princes had gathered there from all parts of the country. Draupadi entered the hall with her brother Dhrishtadyumna. Many noted princes like Sisupala, Jarasandha, Salya, Duryodhana tried in vain to string the bow, but it was too heavy and stiff for them and they returned to their places. Then Arjuna who had come disguised as a Brahmin stood up, meditated the Supreme God and took the bow in his hand and strung it with ease. He placed an arrow on the string and without hesitation he shot five arrows in succession through the revolving mechanism right into the target so that it fell down. Draupadi placed the garland in Arjuna's neck. Krishna and Balram were also present there, and happy to see Arjun there.

Pandavas along with Draupadi reached their temporary house of potter. When the Pandavas reached their house, Arjuna asked her mother who was inside the hut to guess what he had brought for her, as he wanted to give her a surprise, but Kunti told him whatever he had brought, he would distribute among his other brothers. But when she came out of the hut, she was astonished to see the beautiful Draupadi. Then Arjuna told her mother that he could not break her pledge that all the brothers would share all of the things in common. Draupada also came to know that he married her daughter to the five Pandavas because rishi Vyas had already told him that Draupadi had got the boon of five husbands from Lord Shiva.

The news of the marriage of Draupadi spread all over. Vidur informed Dhritarashtra that all the Pandavas are alive and they married the daughter of Draupada. On hearing Vidur's words, Dhritarashtra sent Vidur to Raja Draupad to bring back the Pandavas and their mother. When the Pandavas reached Hastinapur, people welcomed them warmly. Dhritarashtra gave half the kingdom to Pandavas and Yudhishtra was crowned the king and he told them to make Khandavaprastha as their capital. The settlement was done in order to avoid hatred between the Pandavas and the Kauravas. The Pandavas renovated that ruined city, built palaces, forts and renamed it Indraprastha. The Pandavas ruled there happily.

One day Narad Muni came to Indraprastha and asked Draupadi, being the wife of the five Pandavas, was there any rule to live with them? On hearing Naradji, the Pandavas made a rule that each brother would live with Draupadi for a month and whoever would break it, would be sent for twelve years to the jungle. One day Arjuna was sitting outside when a Brahmin came and he told Arjuna that someone had taken his cows and he had to help him. Arjuna's bow and and arrows were inside the room where Yudhishthira and Draupti were. Arjuna went inside the room and took his weapons and saved the cows of the Brahmin. Since he broke the rule, he was sent for twelve years to the jungle. Arjuna roamed many cities and he married Chitrangda, the princess of Manipur. Then he reached Dwarka where Krishna welcomed him. On the advice of Krishna, he married Subhadra. After completing the twelve years, he came back to Indraprastha.

Subhadra gave birth to Abhimanyu. Draupadi also gave birth to five sons.

Sabha Parva

The Pandavas ruled Indraprastha in all glory. One day Naradji visited Indraprastha and urged Yudhishthira to perform the *Rajasurya yagya*. Yudhishthira sought Lord Krishna's advice in this matter, therefore called him from Dwarka. Krishna told Yudhishthira that there was no doubt that he could perform *Rajasurya* but Jarasandha of Magadha had conquered many kings, including Sisupla (afraid of his power) and were submissive to him. Krishna made a plan to eliminate Jarasandha who was the only obstacle to oppose Yudhishtra from becoming an emperor, by making Bhima, a wrestler with Jarasandha.

Yudhishthira became upset on hearing Krishna but Bhima and Arjuna encouraged him. Krishna, Bhima and Arjuna reached the court of Jarasandha disguised as brahmins. After aquainting himself as to who the brahmins were, Jarasandha said that since Bhima is famous for his physical strength, he, therefore, wanted to fight with him. Both fought continuously for thirteen days but on the fourteenth day Jarasandha showed signs of exhaustion and Krishna prompted Bhima that the time had come to make an end of him. Bhima tore Jarasandha and threw the two portions in opposite directions so that they could not come together and join. After the death of Jarasundha, the way was clear for the *Rajasurya yagya* which the Pandavas performed with great pomp. Bhisma, Dhritarashtra, Vidur, Dronacharya, Kripacharya, Aswathama, Duryodhana, Duhsasara, etc. came to attend Rajasurya from Indraprastha. The time came for the custom to render first honour to the guest who was considered worthiest of taking precedence over all others and it was decided that Sri Krishna, the king of Dwarka should be honoured first. Under Yudhishthira's instructions, Sahadeva offered to Sri Krishna the honours enjoined by tradition. Sisupala, the king of Chedi and son of Krishna's bua hated Krishna, could not tolerate it. Krishna promised his bua that he would excuse Sisupala for his hundered crimes. Sisupala spoke harsh words to Krishna then Krishna killed Sisupala with his *Sudershan Chakra* and made his son the king of Chedi.

On seeing the prosperity of the Pandavas, Duryodhana was burning with jealousy, he started making plans with Sakuni, his uncle/mama. Sakuni advised him that he knew the way to drive Yudhishthira out of Indraprastha without a fight. They would invite the Pandavas for the game of dice and Yudhishthira being unskillful and ignorant of the tricks of the game and he (sakuni) knowing the tricks of the game, would win his kingdom and wealth without shedding any blood.

They were sure that Yudhishthira following the tradition of the Kshatriyas would not turn down their invitation for the game. Duryodhana also convinced Dhritarashtra for inviting the Pandavas for the game of the dice and ordered for a new hall to be built for that game. When Vidura came to know of that game, he told Dhritarashtra that the game would bring the ruin of their race by raising unquenchable hate, but Dhritarashtra could not oppose the demands of his son and ordered Vidura to invite the Pandavas for the game of dice on his behalf. Vidura went to Yudhishthira with an invitation. All the Pandavas along with Draupadi came to Hastinapur. Duhsasana announced that the game would be between Yudhishthira and Duryodhana, and mama Sakuni would cast the dice on his behalf. The hall was fully crowded, Dronacharya, Kripacharya, Bhishma, Vidura and Dhritarashtra were also seated there. They knew that the game would end viciously and sat unhappily witnessing what they could not prevent. At first, they wagered jewels and later gold, silver and then chariots and horses. Yudhishthira lost continuously. Yudhishthira staked his servants, elephants, armies and lost them too. He then offered his brothers and himself but lost all. Then Sakuni told Yudhishthira that he still had one jewel left in his possession and by staking which, he could free himself, therefore, could offer his wife Draupadi as wager. There was audible distress and agitation in that part of the assembly where the elders sat. Sakuni cast the dice and he won.

Hall of Assembly

Duryodhana turned to Vidura and told him to go and fetch Draupadi, the beloved wife of the Pandavas who would sweep and clean their house. Vidur turned to the assembly and addressed them saying that Yudhishthira had no right to stake Draupadi/Panchali as by then he had himself already lost his freedom and lost all rights. He was seeing or foresaw

Draupadi dragged in Kaurvas Assembly

the ruin of the Kauravas. Duryodhana became angry at Vidur's words, therefore, sent Vikarna, his brother to bring

Draupadi. He told her the whole story how Yudhishthira had lost all his wealth and had finally bet her after having first forefeited his brothers and himself. She asked him when Yudhishthira lost himself first, then how did he get the right to stake her? She requested him to raise her question before the assembly because she didn't belong to him alone. He repeated the question of Draupadi in the assembly, Yudhishthira was shocked to hear him. Duryodhana then sent Duhsasana who caught her by the hair and dragged her to the assembly. Bhishma, Vidur, Dronacharya and Kripacharya could not bear the sight of the agony of Panchali. Seeing the tears of Draupadi, Bhima took the vow that he would tear the hands of Duhsasana with which he touched the hair of Draupadi. Kauravas became afraid at hearing Bhima's pledge but Duryodhana showed his thighs and asked Draupadi to sit on it. Seeing this, Bhima shouted loudly that Duryodhana was insulting Draupadi by patting his thighs, he would break his thighs with his *gada*. Then Duryodhana asked Duhasasana that since Draupadi had become our maid, her clothes would be seized. Duhasasana went to Draupadi and made ready to seize her clothes by force. Draupadi requested everyone present in the assembly to save her from that insult but nobody came to her rescue and all bent down their heads. At last, she rémembered Krishna for her refuge and protection and she fainted. Then a miracle occurred. People saw as Duhasasana was pulling off her garments, fresh garments were seen to clothe her body and soon a great heap of resplendent clothes were piled up till Duhasasana sat down in sheer fatigue. Then Bhima took a pledge/oath that he would not go to the blessed abode of his ancestors till he did not tear the breast and drink the heart's blood of sinful Duhasasana.

The people sitting in the assembly became afraid on hearing Bhima's pledge. Dhritarashtra also realised that the incident would be the cause of destruction of his race and for once, acted with wisdom and courage. He called Draupadi to his side and attempted to soothe her and told Yudhishthira to take back his kingdom, riches and everything else and be free and prosperous and return to Indraprastha.

After Yudhishthira and his brothers had left, there was a long discussion and incited by Duhasasana, Sakuni and others, Duryodhana got his father's consent once again to play a game of dice. A messenger was despatched who invited Yudhishthira on behalf of Dhritarashtra. There was one change and that was that the defeated party would go with his brothers into exile to the forest for twelve years and spend the thirteenth year incognito and if they would be recognized during the thirteenth year, they would go into exile for another twelve years. Dhritarashtra did not like the purpose of playing the dice again but he yielded to the desire of his son.

Yudhishthira along with his brothers returned to Hastinapur and the game was started again with Sakuni. Everyone in the assembly tried to dissuade him but he seemed a mere pawn moved by destiny. Yudhishthira was again defeated in the game and as per conditions, he along with his brothers and wife had to go to the forest for thirteen years.

Van Parva

After leaving Kunti in Vidur's house, the Pandavas along with Draupadi left for exile for twelve years and one year incognito. The people of their kingdom also wanted to accompany them, but all of them came back on the request of Yudhishthira except the brahmins. After reaching the jungle, Yudhishthira worshipped Surya, who after becoming happy with him gave him an *Akshyapatra*, a wonderful vessel which held a never failing supply of food (from which food was never finished). Draupadi would first offer the food to the brahmins and then to the Pandavas and at last she used to eat. After roaming in the jungle, they reached Kamiyaka jungle on the shores of the Saraswati river.

Draupad and Krishna were not happy on hearing the news about the Pandavas. They met Vyasa muni in the jungle who advised Arjuna to go to the Himalayas to practise austerities for the purpose of getting new weapons from the *devas*.

Accordingly, he prayed to Shiva who gave him the *Gandiva* as well as other weapons (of which he had been deprived). He also bestowed on Arjuna the marvellous *Pasupata* weapon. After that, he came to the kingdom of gods who also gave their weapons to him.

Karna was also jealous of the Pandavas. He prayed to God to defeat Arjuna. Seeing his *tapaysa*, Indra became worried because he wanted to help Arjuna. Disguised as a Brahmin, Indra went to Karna and asked for his divine armour and earrings. Since Karna was the son of Surya/ sun god, he warned Karna before Indra asked for his armour and earrings. But being giving was his nature, he cut off the armour from his body and gave his earrings to Indra. Indra was very pleased to see Karna's *dan shakti* and gave him amogh sakti/a power and told him that whenever he would use this power, that person would definitely die and after that the power would return to him. After that Indra vanished.

The stipulated period of twelve years of the Pandavas

was drawing to a close, and the thought of one year of incognito was worrying them. One day, they went far away while chasing a deer on the request of a Brahmin who wanted to perform the fire sacrifice. They became thirsty. Nakul went in search of water, he saw a pool and thought of quenching his thirst first before taking water for his brothers but as soon as his hands touched the water, he heard a voice saying this pool belongs to me, answer my questions and then drink the water. Due to his intense thirst and heedless of the warning, he drank the water and fell down. When Nakul did not turn up, Sahadeva came but he too did not pay heed to the warning and drank the water and dropped down. Then Yudhishthira sent Arjuna who saw both of his brothers lying dead near the pool. He also quenched his thirst first and faced the same consequence. Then Bhima came, saw his brothers, did not pay heed to the voice and drank the water, faced the same end.

Yudhishthira became worried about his brothers, he then proceeded in the direction his brothers had taken and reached near the pool and saw his four brothers lying dead. He heard the same voice saying that his brothers died because they did not pay heed to his words, answer the questions first, then quench your thirst. Yudhishthira knew that the voice could be none other than the words of Yaksha and he agreed to answer his questions.

Yaksha – What rescues man in danger?

Yudhishthira – Courage

Yaksha – What is that abandoning which man becomes loved by all?

Yudhishthira - Pride

Yaksha – What is the loss which yields joy and not sorrow?

Yudhishthira – Anger

Yaksha – What is that, by giving up which, man becomes rich?

Yudhishthira – Desire.

Yaksha – What makes one a real *Brahmana*? Is it birth, good conduct or learning?

Yudhishthira – Good conduct

Yaksha – What is greater than *Dharma* in the world?

Yudhishthira – Virility

Yaksha – What is happiness?

Yudhishthira – It is the result of good conduct

Yaksha – Who accompanies a man in death?

Yudhishthira – Dharma

Yaksha – Which is the biggest vessel?

Yudhishthira – The Earth

Yaksha – What is the loss which yields joy and not sorrow?

Yudhishthira – Anger (giving it up, we will no longer be subject to sorrow)

Yaksha – What is higher than the sky?

Yudhishthira – Father

Yaksha – What is fleeter than wind?

Yudhishthira – Mind

Yaksha – What befriends a traveller?

Yudhishthira – learning

Yaksha – What is more blighted than withered straw?

Yudhishthira – A sorrow stricken heart

Thus, Yaksha posed many questions and Yudhishthira answered them all. In the end, Yaksha asked Yudhishthira one of his dead brothers could be revived and whom did he want to revive.

Yudhishthira took the name of Nakul. As Kunti and Madri were the two wives of my father, he was surviving as a son of Kunti and Nakul would survive as a son of Madri. Yaksha was pleased to hear Yudhishthira's impartiality and granted that all his brothers would come back to life. It was Yama, the Lord of death, who had taken the form of Yaksha and deer, so that he could see his son Yudhishthira and test him.

Virat Parva

The twelve years of exile of the Pandavas passed but they were worried about the thirteenth year of exile as they had to spend the twelve months undiscovered by the spies of Duryodhana. They discussed their future line of action and decided to go to the kingdom of Virata, the king of Matsya, who was a strong king and was not afraid of Duryodvana. When they went to king Virata seeking service he appointed Yudhishthira as his companion and spent his days in playing dice with him. Bhima worked as the chief of cooks, Arjuna assumed the name of Brihannala and taught dancing, singing and instrumental music to princess Uttara, the daughter of Virata. Nakula looked after the horses and Sachdeva looked after the cows and bulls and Draupadi would serve Sudeshna, the queen of Virata. She lived in the inner apartments of the palace as maid Sairandhri.

Kichaka, the brother of Sudeshna, who was the commander-in-chief of Virata's army became influenced by the beauty of Draupadi and started making futile advances towards her. Frightened Sairandhri requested Kichaka that she was an ordinary married maid, therefore, he must not behave like that with her. Being influenced by her brother Kichaka, Sudeshna sent Sairandhri to him to bring something from him. When she reached his room, he became mad with lust and pestered her with solicitations. She ran away to

Bhima and told him everything. Bhima killed him at night in the dancing hall. The news of Kichaka's death spread that Sairandhri's husband had killed him.

From the beginning of the thirteenth year, the spies of Duryodhana had searched for the Pandavás but in vain. On hearing the news of Kichaka's death, King Susarna, the ruler of Trigarta and a friend of Duryodhana thought of attacking King Virata thinking that Kichaka's death must have weakened Virata. Susarna invaded Matsya and seized the cattles, the cowherds ran in great distress to Virata for help. Yudhishthira promised to help Virat. All the Pandavas excepting Arjuna went out with the army of Virata to oppose Susarana. Susarna captured Virata and held him captive in his chariot but Bhima attacked the enemy and set Virata free and captured Susarna. The army of Duryodhana including Bhisma, Dronacharya, Kripacharya, Karna and Aswathama attacked and rounded up the countless cows that were there. Brihannala became a charioteer of Uttara, the son of Virata. Seeing the army of Kauravas, Uttara Kumar asked Brihannala to turn back the chariot but Brihannala took down the arms hidden in the tree, meditated on his armour, got into the chariot and gloried in the familiar feel of his *Gandiva* vow.

Uttara Kumar moved his chariot in front of the large army of Kauravas. There were great fights with them in which Vikarma was killed, Karna was also wounded, Bhishma and Dronacharya fell down unconscious when Arjuna employed a magic weapon. The whole army returned to Hastinapur after a humiliating defeat.

When Virata king came to know about the reality of the Pandavas and Draupadi, he became very happy and promised them his help. He decided to marry his daughter Uttara to Abhimanyu, son of Arjuna.

Udyog Parva

The thirteenth year during which the Pandavas had to remain undiscovered came to an end but the feeling of revenge from the Kauravas was still there. Sri Krishna advised the Pandavas that they should make preparations for the war. They called all the kings to the capital of Virat, Draupada, the king of Panchala and the father of Draupadi and Virata promised to help the Pandavas. Duryodhana came to know about the Pandava's plan, therefore, all the kings helping Kauravas and Pandavas came to Kurushetra after collecting their forces in readiness for war.

Both Duryodhana and Arjuna went to Dwarka seeking Krishna's help. When both reached, Krishna was sleeping. Duryodhana who went first seated himself on a chair at the head of the bed and Arjuna kept standing at Krishna's feet. When Krishna woke up, he welcomed both and asked them what brought them to Dwarka. Explaining about the circumstances of war, Arjuna seeked Krishna's support. Duryodhana told Krishna that as per tradition, he who came first should be given the preference. Then Krishna explained that both of them were his relatives and equal to him. He had two options for them – his *Narayani* army and he himself who would weild no weapon and take no part in the battle. Arjuna chose Krishna alone but Duryodhana chose Vasudeva's army.

Duryodhana deceived Salya, the ruler of Madradesa, brother of Madri, the mother of Nakul and Sahadeva. He was forced to make a promise to Duryodhana that he and his forces would fight on Duryodhana's side. Salya who met the Pandavas, narrated their hardships and sufferings. Yudhishthira took a promise from him that in case he would become the charioteer of Karna in the battle and if Karna made an attempt to attack Arjuna, he would save Arjuna.

Krishna who came from Dwarka to know what Duryodhana had told Draupada's Brahmana messenger that he would not give a needle point of territory to the Pandavas. Yudhishthira was even ready to make a treaty with the Kauravas by taking only five villages and he requested Krishna to go to Hastinapur with the said proposal.

Dhritarashtra issued orders for making arrangements to receive Krishna. Krishna first visited Dhritarashtra, then proceeded to Vidur's house, where he met Kunti. Next day, Krishna reached the court of the Kauravas with the Pandava's proposal and advised Dhritarashtra to pursue the path of *dharma* and not to bring ruin to his people as war was not advisable. In war, the Kshatriyas would be killed and truth and dharma/religion would be perished. Pandavas were deceived in the game of dice arranged as a conspiracy by Duryodhana and Sakuni. They suffered twelve years of exile and one year of incognito and Draupadi was insulted in the court assembly of the Kauravas. In spite of all these sufferings, Yudhishthira wanted to live peacefully with his family after taking half of the kingdom. Duryodhana told Krishna that instead of doing the work of emissary, he was taking the side of the Pandavas. Being the eldest son of Dhritarashtra, he was considered as an heir to the throne. Since Krishna was on the side of Pandavas, he was also responsible for all of that. Duryodhana and his friends plotted to seize Krishna, who anticipated all this, laughed and disclosed his divinity.

Krishna narrated all the incidents that happened in the court of Hastinapur to Kunti. She met Karna and told him the truth about his birth that he was the son of Surya and how he was born and that he was a brother of the Pandavas. She gave him her blessings and requested him not to fight with the Pandavas but he assured her that either he or Arjuna would die in the war. He would not kill her other sons. Either he or Arjuna would survive, and with the other four sons, she would still have five sons. When Kunti heard this, her heart became full of tumultuous emotions and contrary feelings, she embraced Karna.

Krishna reached the Pandavas and told them what had happened in Hastinapur and everyone presumed it was an evident. Meanwhile, Rishi Vyas visited Dhritarashtra and he expressed his desire to see the war. Rishi Vyas gave Sanjay Divya eyes by which he could explain to Dhritarashtra all the incidents of the battle sitting near him.

Sanjay explaining to Dhritarashtra the details of the battle at Kurushetra

Bhishma Parva

Both the armies of Kauravas and Pandavas stood face to face in Kurukshetra. Bhishma was the commander of the Kaurava army. Arjuna was in front of the Pandavas army and Krishna was driving his chariot. When Arjuna saw Bhishma, Dronacharya, Kripacharya, Aswatthama, Duryodhana, Duhsasana and other relatives standing in front of him in the battlefield, he became grieved and was thinking that he would have to kill all his relatives first and then get the kingdom to rule. In order to achieve this, many people would

Krishna driving the chariot of Arjuna

be killed, women become widows and children would be orphaned, then what would he do for such a state. He put his *Gandiva* down and sat down in dismay. Then Krishna spoke to Arjuna in order to quell his agitation and remove his doubts

Krishna speaking to Arjuna in roder to quell his agitation and remove his doubts

and Krishna's exhortation to Arjuna at that juncture is called the Bhagvad Gita, which is enshrined in millions of hearts in the world. Krishna showed Arjuna his *Virata Rupa*, his attachment with his kith and kin vanished and he became ready for the war.

Krishna sharing his Virat Rupa to Arjuna

The battle began, on the first day of battle, the Pandava's army was badly shaken. Wherever Bhishma's chariot went, it was like the dance of the destroyer. On the second day, the Pandavas army was most carefully arrayed and they fought with confidence, not repeating the mistakes of the first day.

Announcement of the battle

Third day, Bhishma led the army in an eagle formation, Drona and Bhishma jointly attacked Yudhishthira. Nakul and Sahadeva joined their brother in opposing Drona's offensive. Their army was badly demoralised.

On the fourth day, Bhima killed eight of Duryodhana's brothers and his arrows would have killed Duryodhana too. Ghatotkacha, the son of Bhima got angry and fell on the Kauravas army. On the fifth day, Arjuna killed thousands of warriors and both the armies retired to camp along with the tired horses and elephants. During the sixth day, Dronacharya's charioteer was killed and he took the reins of the horses himself. He killed Dhirishtadyumna's charioteer and horses and smashed his chariot. On the eighth day, the battle was fought simultaneously at many sectors. Bhishma personally opposed Arjuan's attack, Duryodhana and Dhirishtadyumna fought with each other and so on. On the eighth day, sixteen of Duryodhana's brothers perished. On the ninth day, Bhishma fought furiously and beat the Pandavas back, their forces were demoralised and were fleeing hither and thither. Seeing this, Krishna advised Arjuna to attack Bhishma keeping Sikhandi (Draupada's son) in front of him. Bhishma decided not to be provoked into fighting with Sikandi whom he knew was born a woman and to strike him was unworthy of a warrior.

Seeing Srikhandi, Bhishma laid down his bow and Arjuna pierced him. He fell from his chariot, not on the ground but on a bed of the arrows with which he had been transfixed. Since he had taken the vow of celibacy, he had received the gift of choosing the time of his death, so he preferred to lie on his bed of arrows through to the end of the war.

Bhishma's body on the arrows of Arjuna

Drona Parva

After Bhishma, Dronacharya took the command of the battle. He was everywhere in the field and displayed the fierce energy of a warrior. Whenever he led an attack, the Pandava forces were scattered like clouds before a storm. He fought Bhima, Arjuna, Dhrishtadyumna, Abhimanyu, Drupada etc. He inflicted severe punishment on the Pandava army during the five days he was in command. The Pandava forces also attacked Drona's army and brought great havoc and the twelfth day's fight ended.

Yudhishthira got the news of *chakravue* battle on the thirteenth day. He became worried because Krishna and Arjuna were far away from them and his army did not know how to break Dronacharya's array. Abhimanyu who was there told them that he had been instructed by his father on how to penetrate that array when he was in the womb of his mother but he did not know how to come out from that because when the father Arjuna explained it, the mother, Subhadra had slept. Being Krishna's nephew and son of Arjuna, fear did not approach him and he approached near the Kaurava army, the formation was breached and Abhimanyu entered. But the breach closed under the inspiration of Jayadratha, king of the Sindhu before the other Pandavas could force their way, thus Abhimanyu was alone. Kaurava warriors opposed him but they fell like moths in the fire, one after another. Seeing the destruction wrought by him, Dronacharya, Aswathama, Kripacharya, Karna, Sakuni, Salya equipped with all arms, surged an attack on Abhimanyu. His horses and charioteer were killed, thus he stood alone with his sword and shield in the battlefield. He fought fiercely with the discus, one of his chariot wheels after his sword and shield were broken by Dronacharya and Karna. Abhimanyu, single handedly wrecked havoc on the Kaurava army, was overpowered by all and killed cruelly.

The Pandavas plunged in sorrow after hearing of the death of Abhimanyu. Arjuna took an oath to slay Jayadratha before the sunset of the next day who caused his son's death and he killed him on the fourteenth day. Ghatotkacha, son of Bhima destroyed thousands of the army of the Kauravas, seeing which Duryodhana's heart sank and he asked Karna to kill him. Karna had with him the spear of unerring effect which Indra gave him and which could be used once and which he kept for Arjuna. But Karna was impelled by a sudden urge and hurled the missile at Ghatotkacha who died. Bhima lifted his iron mace and brought it down on the head of a huge elephant called Aswatthama and it fell dead.

On the fifteenth day, Dhrishtadhyumna, the son of Draupad and brother of Draupadi attacked Dronacharya in order to take the revenge but he was not able to bear the rain of his arrows. Krishna also became worried to see Dronacharya's mode of fighting and thought that the death of Dronacharya was necessary for the victory of the Pandavas. He told Arjuna to inform Dronacharya that Aswatthama died and there was truth in it since Bhima had killed an elephant called Aswatthama. Dronacharya heard the words when he was in the act of discharging a brahmastra. He enquired with Yudhishthira who confirmed the news but added in a low voice that it was an elephant which was not heard. After hearing the news of the death of his son, his attachment to life snapped. He threw his weapon away and sat down in yoga on the floor of his chariot. At that moment Dhrishtadyumna came and swept off his head.

The news of the death of Dronacharya spread and the Kauravas became distressed. Aswatthama got angry and made attempts on Pandavas. By evening, the war was stopped.

Karna Parva

After the death of Dronacharya, Karna became the commander of the Kauravas army and Salya drove his chariot. He took pledge to eliminate the Pandavas. On the sixteenth day of the battle, Arjuna led the attack on Karna supported by Bhima. Bhima tore Duhsasana's arm out and threw the bleeding limb on the battlefield. Thus, he fulfilled the terrible oath he had taken thirteen years ago. Everyone was shaken including Karna. Karna with eyes red and unshed tears asked Salya to drive his chariot towards Arjuna. Then followed a great battle. The son of Surya, Karna, sent a dazzling arrow like a serpant with its flaming double tongue out. Then Krishna, Arjuna's charioteer at the nick of time, pressed Karna's chariot five fingers deep in the mud so that the serpent shaft just missed Arjuna's head but swept off his helmet. Arjuna in anger fixed a dart on his bow to make an end of Karna. He jumped down on the ground to lift the wheel up from the mud, Arjuna on the command of Krishna sent an arrow which cut and severed his head from the body. After the death of Karna, Duryodhana made Salya the commander of the Kaurava army.

Salya Parva

On the side of the Pandavas, Yudhishthira led the attack personally against Salya. On the Kauravas side, there were Duryodhana, Kripacharya, Aswatthama and Kritavarma, a notable Yadava warrior left. Yudhishthira hurled at Salya, his spear went straight, struck him and he died. When Salya fell dead, Kauravas lost all hope. Sakuni led the attack on Sahadeva, who discharged a sharp-edged sword array which went straight and cut through his neck, which rolled on the ground. Left alone, Duryodhana took up his mace and walked towards a pool of water. Yudhishthira and his brothers arrived there, he stepped out of the pool and a fight began between him and Bhima. Krishna instigated Bhima to aim his blow on Duryodhana's thigh. Meanwhile Balarama arrived at Kurukshetra after completing his tour of holy places. He saw Bhima give a deadly blow below the navel which broke Duryodhana's thigh and his anger flamed up because of the breach of the rules. Then Krishna intervened and explained to him all the incidents which took place which led to their miseries. Duryodhana fell down on the ground. When Kripacharya, Aswatthama and Kritavarma came to know about Duryodhana's condition, they reached him.

Duryodhana cried in distress that the Pandavas killed the great warriors of his army like Bhishma, Jayadrath, Dronacharya, Karna, Salya, etc. by foul play and started crying. He was in the last physical agony of departing life, he ordered to install Aswatthama as the supreme commander of the army who promised Duryodhana to take revenge from the Pandavas and send them to the abode of Yama.

Saptik Parva

Aswatthama made up his mind with a plan and woke up Kripacharya and Kritavarma. They reached the Pandava's camp. Dhirishtadyumna was sleeping in his tent. Aswatthama leapt on him and before he could put himself into a posture of defence, cruelly kicked him to death. The same process was repeated until all the sons of Draupadi were killed one by one when they were plunged in sleep in their tents. After this heinous deed, they came out of the tents and set fire to the camp. When the fire spread, the sleeping soldiers were awakened and fled here and there in confusion. Then they reached Duryodhana and Aswatthama told him that they had slaughtered the Pandavas, Dhirishtadyumna, Sikhandi, Panchalya (son of king Draupada) and had brought Pandavas heads. Hearing that, Duryodhana's heart became gladdened and he requested for the head of Bhima in spite of all his sufferings. He gave a big blow with his hand to the head but it broke, only then he realised that it was not the head of Bhima. When dawn broke, he saw all the five heads and realised that they were not the heads of Pandavas but were of Draupadi's sons and with great grief Duryodhana died. Draupadi was inconsolable to see the death of her sons. The Pandavas went out in search of Aswatthama and found him. When he saw the Pandavas and Krishna approaching, he took up a blade of grass and charged it with a *mantra* of destruction and sent it forward to destroy the race of the Pandavas. It went straight to the womb of Uttara who bore in her the son of Abhimanyu. The race of the Pandavas would be destroyed thereby but for the mercy of Krishna who saved the child in the mother's womb. This child was Parikshit who was later crowned by Yudhishthira when the Pandavas retired to the forest. Aswatthama prised out the shinning jewel which was part of his head, gave it to Bhima acknowledging his defeat and went away to the forest.

Other Parvas

There were other Parvas also besides the Parvas mentioned above. They are Stri parva, Shanti parva, Anushashan parva, Ashvamega parva, Ashram Mausala parva, Mahaprathanik parva and Swargarohan parva. The details of the said parvas were like that – after the death of Duryodhana, Hastinapur became the city of mourning as the women were weeping because of their near and dearest being slained. Bhanimati, wife of Duryodhana fainted, Gandhari cried bitterly, Dhritarashtra fainted and Vidur also cried. Dhritarashtra and others went to Kurukshtera and saw the scene of destruction.

When the Pandavas came to know that Dhritarashtra and others proceeded towards Kurukshtera, they too went there to meet them. Dhritarashtra told everyone that *dharma* had won, where there was *adharma*, there would be no victory and so it had happened, all his army was finished. Bhima alone killed my sons, he asked to embrace Bhima who killed Duryodhana. Krishna knew that, therefore, he pushed Bhima aside and placed an iron figure before Dhritarashtra knowing his anger against Bhima. Dhritarashtra hugged the metal statue to his bosom in a firm embrace and then the thought came to him of how Bhima killed his sons, and his wrath increased to such a pitch that the statue was crushed to pieces and he cried that his anger had killed Bhima. Then Krishna told him that he did not kill Bhima but crushed only an iron image which he (Krishna) placed before him. Dhritarashtra became ashamed of his deeds. Then Krishna along with the Pandavas went to Gandhari and consoled her, after that all of them went to Kurukshetra. Gandhari suppressed all her anger but gave a curse to Krishna that he finished their dynasty, she cursed him that his dynasty would also be finished in the same way as theirs.

After the battle of Kurukshetra, Yudhishthira's pain of mind increased every day as he thought of all the kinsman who had been killed. He was stricken with intense remorse and decided to give up the world, go to the forest and do penance to expiate his sins. But at the instigation of Vyasa sage, he was crowned and installed as king. He went to Bhishma with hesitation and requested him to give teachings on religion and discipline. He went to Bhishma regularly and made use of his teachings. Bhishma who was on the bed of arrow for fifty-eight days, now decided to leave and died. Yudhishthira made the pyre of sandalwood and lit it.

Yudhishthira ruled over Hastinapur and discharged his duties according to *dharma*. Dhritarashtara and Gandhari who were plunged into grief were treated by the Pandavas with utmost respect. They did nothing to humiliate them. After sometime the wife of Abhimanyu, Uttara, gave birth to a still child but by the grace of Krishna he became alive and he was named as Parikshit.

Yudhishthira performed an *Aswamedha* yajna, great horse sacrifice and as per customs all the princes were invited and everything was done in a magnificent style. Thus passed the fifteen years. At the instigation of Vyasa and (the *dharma* of kings is to die in battle or to spend their last days of retirement in the forest) as per customs Dhritarashtra, Gandhari, Sanjay, Kunti and Vidur left for the forest. They spent three years in the forest. When one day the forest caught fire, the wind blew and the flames spread everywhere, the three Dhritarashtara, Gandhari and Kunti sat down on the ground and calmly gave themselves up to the flames.

Krishna reached Dwarka after the Kurukshetra battle was over. He became famous for his rule but the Yadavas used to spend their time in unrestrained self-indulgence and luxury. They became indisciplined and inhuman. Soon, all the Yadavas were in a quarrel on one side or the other. Satyaki, with this sword drawn, sprang upon Kritavarma and swept his head off. Pradyumna, son of Krishna, tried to rescue Satyaki but both of them got killed. Krishna knew that the destined hour had come. Seeing all that, Balarama gave up his life as he laid in a yoga trance and passed away into the ocean. With the passing of Balarama, and seeing his people destroying themselves, he went in deep meditation under a pipal tree. Meanwhile, a hunter came, mistook Krishna as a wild animal from the distance, shot an arrow at Krishna piercing his foot in the instep and thus he left the world.

When the Pandavas came to know about the demise of Krishna, they lost all attachment to life on earth. They crowned Parikshit, son of Abhimanyu as the emperor and left the kingdom with Draupadi. After visiting holy places, they reached the Himalayas. A dog joined them somewhere and kept them company all along. Draupadi fell down and died, after her Sahadeva, Nakula, Arjuna and Bhima also fell one by one and died. Only Yudhishthira along with the dog was left. When he reached at a great height, Indra appeared in his chariot and asked Yudhishthira to ascend his chariot but his dog was not allowed in *Swarga*, upon that Yudhishthira refused to go to heaven. *Dharma* in the body of dog had come to test Yudhishthira's loyalty and he was pleased with his conduct and the dog vanished from sight.

Indra took Yudhishthira to *Swarga* where he saw

Kauravas but not his brothers. Then he asked Indra about the whereabouts of his brothers. On the instruction of Indra, a messenger came and Yudhishthira followed him to hell, where he saw his brothers and Draupadi. Overwhelmed by anger, Yudhishthira turned to the attendant and asked him to go to Indra and he would stay there where his dear brothers and Draupadi were consigned to the torture of the hell. At that time Indra and Yama, the God of *dharma* appeared before Yudhishthira, smiled at him and said that they tested him for the third time, it was just an illusion designed to test him. It was not hell but Swarga. Yudhishthira became very happy to see his brothers and others in *Swarga*. He too left his body and attained the state of the gods.

❑

RAM CHARITA MANAS

7
Ram Charita Manas

Sri Ram Charita Manas is considered one of the vital epics of Hindu religion. This epic was created and written by Goswami Tulsidas, son of Shri Atmaram Dubey and Smt. Tulsi Devi.

There is a famous story behind the creation of Ramcharita Manas – once Tulslidas's wife Smt. Ratna Devi went to spend a few days with her parents. As Tulsidas was missing his wife, he followed her to her parent's house. Seeing Tulsidas at the door, his wife condemned him and said – "if you would have dedicated half of the love that you have for me towards the Almighty, you would have achieved the ultimate truth." Her words caused a great effect on Tulsidas and he immediately left for Kashi. One day, Lord Shiva and Parvati appeared in his dreams and asked him to go to Ayodhya and write an epic. Following Lord Shiva's instructions, Tulsidas reached Ayodhya and wrote an epic named Ramcharita Manas. The epic was written in two years, seven months and twent-seven days and completed on the Birthday of Lord Rama, viz. – ninth day of Chaitra month, according to the Hindu calendar.

The epic provides guidelines on an ideal family life (*parivarik Jeevan or grahastha Jeevan*), an ideal king (*raj dharma*) and an ideal mother (*matra dharma*). In addition, the epic also talks about devotion – *bhakti*, knowledge – *gyan*, renunciation – *vairagya* and good behaviour – *sadachar*. Here is the story of Ramcharita Manas that was told by Lord Shiva to Parvati and was also narrated by Kakbhushundji to Garudji – the king of the birds. Sri Ramcharita Manas is divided into seven sections, viz. Bal Kand, Ayodhya Kand, Arayana Kand, Kishikandha Kand, Sundar Kand, Lanka Kand, and Uttar Kand, the details of which are as follows:

Bal Kand

(This section tells the story of the birth of Lord Rama till his marriage with Sita.) There was a king named Raja Dashratha, who ruled Ayodhya. He had three queens, namely Kaushalya, Kakayi and Sumitra. Queen Kaushalya gave birth to Rama, Kakayi to Bharat and Sumitra to Lakshman and Shatrughan. When the four brothers grew up, the thread ceremony was performed and they were sent to the Ashram of sage Vishwamitra for studies. Since Vishwamitra knew that

Sri Rama as a child

Rama has taken birth in order to kill the demons and make the earth free from their menace, he, therefore, went to King Dashratha and said – "O King, the demons do not allow me to perform oblations peacefully in the forest, I therefore, request you to send both Rama and Lakshman along with me

Rama playing with Crow

so that they would kill the demons and make me free from their menace." King Dashratha acceded to the request of sage Vishwamitra and sent Rama and Lakshman along with him. On the way, Rama killed Taraka an asur, Subahu and Marich and made the brahmins free from their menace. On the way, Rama also noticed a statue of a woman and Vishwamitra told Rama that it was sage Gautam's wife Ahilya's statue whom he had converted by a curse. He advised Rama that she would be liberated from the curse when Rama touched her with his feet. Thus, Rama followed the instruction of Vishwamitra and the statue transformed into a woman. She thanked Rama and left for heaven to meet her husband.

On getting the invitation from king Janak, Vishwamitra reached Mithila along with Rama and Lakshman. King Janak organized a swaymvar for her daughter Sita and laid the condition that he will give his daughter's hand to the man who would break Lord Shiva's bow. Everyone present there tried their best but was not successful in accomplishing this difficult task.

Seeing the plight of all participants and misery of Raja Janak, sage Vishwamitra told Rama, "Son! Proceed and break the bow and relieve Raja Janak of his frustration." Seeking blessings from his guru, Lord Rama proceeded towards the stage and lifted the bow and broke it into two pieces. The resulting noise was so loud that it echoed in the entire universe. Realising that Lord Shiva's bow is broken, sage Parshuram was enraged and appeared at the venue, screamed at Raja Janak and asked, "Tell me who broke Lord Shiva's bow, else I will destroy your kingdom."

At this, Lord Rama politely said "I understand your anger but it is a small mistake on my side. Since the bow was very old, it broke as soon as I touched it. I do not take any pride in it." Lord Rama's polite words softened sage Parshuram and he wondered if Rama was an incarnation of Lord Vishnu since it was impossible for anyone else to even lift the bow. To reassure himself, he handed his bow to Rama and was astonished to see that the bow slipped into the hands of Rama. Convinced that Lord Rama was indeed the re-incarnation of Lord Vishnu, sage Parshuram left the venue.

King Janak sent his messengers to Ayodhya to invite king Dashratha and proposed to marry his four daughters to king Dashratha's sons; Lord Rama got married to Sita, Bharat to Mandvi, Lakshman to Urmila and Shatrughan to ShrutiKirti.

Importance: It is believed that those who recite the story of Rama and Sita's marriage will lead a happy and prosperous marital life.

Ayodhya Kand

(This section of Ramcharita Manas demonstrates the crowning ceremony of Lord Rama as the next king of Ayodhya, Kaikayi's demand for the two boons promised to her by king Dashratha, Lord Rama, Lakshman and Sita leaving for the forest and the death of King Dashratha.)

As time passed after the marriage of Lord Rama and king Dashratha was getting old, therefore, he decided to crown Rama as his successor to the throne, so that he may hand over the responsibilities of being the king to Rama. He consulted sage Vashishtha, his minister Sumantha and other members of his court. Everyone was very happy to hear this and accepted it as a blessing from heaven.

However, the *devtas* were worried about this programme. They thought that if Rama was crowned as the king, he would be absorbed in his kingly duties and hence would not have the time to kill the demons. They all gathered and went to Goddess Saraswati to express their worries. The only way that they could be relieved of the demon's torture was if Rama refused from being the king and went to the forest to kill the demons. Goddess Saraswati promised to help the *devtas* by influencing the mind of Kaikayee's maid Manthra, thereby influencing Kaikayee and encouraging her to stop the ceremony of Rama.

Manthra filled the mind of Kaikayee with jealousy and poisoned her against the decision of Lord Rama's coronation. She got very angry and went to kop bhavan. Hearing this, king Dashratha came to cool down her anger, thereupon, Kaikayee demanded the two boons once promised to her by king Dashratha. The story of the two boons was like this – once king Dashratha lost his consciousness during a battle and became wounded, Kaikayee at that time drove his chariot and took him to a safe place and thus saved his life by removing all the arrows from his body. When he gained his consciousness, he became very pleased with her and told her to ask for any boon. Kaikayee did not ask for anything at that time but the king assured her that she could ask for two boons at any time, thus Kaikayee reminded king Dashratha of his two boons as referred above. The first boon which Kaikayee asked was that Rama should be sent for fourteen years to the forest and secondly, her son Bharat should be crowned as the king. Hearing this, king Dashratha got very upset. He tried to reason with Kaikayee but all his efforts were in vain. Since he had given his word to queen Kaikayee, he felt very helpless and at last had to concede to her demands, the sorrow of asking his beloved son Rama to go to the forest was a huge sorrow for him and this affected his health and left him weak and feeble.

Ram, Sita and Lakshman going to the forest

Lord Rama along with Sita and Lakshman took permission from his father and left for the forest in a chariot with Sumantra and reached Tamsa river where Rama offered the evening prayers and Lakshman collected some soft grass so that Rama and Sita could sleep over it. When Lord Rama woke up before dawn, he asked Sumantra to go ahead leaving behind the citizens of Ayodhya. Sumantra drove the chariot and reached Shringwarpur where they met Guha Nishadraj who was the worshipper of Lord Rama. The next morning Lord Rama sent Sumantra back to Ayodhya and reached the banks of the Ganga river along with Sita and Lakshman.

They called for the boat but the ferryman denied to take them across the river and requested Lord Rama politely that he had heard that by the touch of Lord Rama's feet, a stone

Ram, Sita and Lakshman with Kevat crossing the river

was turned into a beautiful woman and if by the touch of Lord Rama's feet, his boat turned into a woman then how would he look after his family, therefore, if Lord Rama wanted to go across the river in his boat, he would allow him to wash his feet first with the Ganga water. Lord Rama accepted his request, then Lord Rama bathed in the Ganga and worshipped Lord Shiva. Next day, after taking a bath in the holy Prayaga, they reached the hermitage of sage Bhardwaj and as per instructions of Balmikiji, they lived in Chitrakoota.

King Dashratha died in the grief of his son Lord Rama and the whole of Ayodhya sank into an ocean of grief. Sage Vashishtha arrived in the palace and ordered to immerse king Dashratha's body in a vessel full of oil till Bharat and Shatrughna arrived from their maternal uncle's palace. Bharat accused his mother Kaikayee after knowing the whole story. He then met Kaushalya who embraced both Bharat and Shatrughana and advised Bharat not to blame anyone, it is all fate. Then Bharat performed the funeral rites of his father king Dashratha according to vedic rites as per orders of Vashishtha and others. Bharat refused to become the king of Ayodhya, instead he wanted that Rama should be crowned as the king, therefore, he went to the forest along with the people of Ayodhya, the three mothers and saints to bring Lord Rama back from Chitrakoota.

Bharat reached the place where Lord Rama, Lakshmana and Sita were staying. After seeing Rama, Bharat fell at his feet and started sobbing. Rama lifted Bharat and embraced him. Sage Vashishtha also met Rama and Lakshman and he informed them about the demise of their father king Dashratha, they all fell into an ocean of grief. Kaikayee was feeling guilty about her ill deed, she fell on Rama's feet and requested him to come to Ayodhya in order to disburse his duties and responsibilities as a king towards the people of Ayodhya. Rama lifted Kaikayee and consoled her that she had not committed any mistake, it is all fate. Parents of Sitaji also reached there. Everybody including Bharat requested Rama to come along to Ayodhya as a king and disburse his duties and responsibilities towards the people of Ayodhya but Rama declined to accompany them because it was his duty to respect the vow which he had given to his late father. He politely told Bharat that it was his dynasty's tradition not to break a promise. Since king Dashratha granted two boons to mother Kaikayee, it became their duty to make them true. Bharat obeyed his orders and requested Rama to give his wooden sandals which he would put as a symbol to rule Ayodhya till Lord Rama's return. Bharat and others returned to Ayodhya.

Importance: Those who will listen to the character of Bharat, will have love and devotion in Lord Rama and Sita and will be inclined towards salvation.

Arandya Kand

(Arandya kaand – the forest episode.)

(This episode relates to the emergence of Shorpanakha, the striking off of the nose and both ears of Shorpanakha by Lakshmana, how Shorpanakha pursued her brothers to fight against Rama and Lakshmana and to take the revenge for her humiliation, how Sita was kidnapped by Ravana, search for Sita by Rama and Lakshman, meeting with Shabari and her information about Sugreeva who would help Rama to find Sita.)

After the departure of Bharat and others, Shri Rama left Chitrakoota and visited the hermitage of saint Atri and his wife Anasuya who blessed them. Anasuya advised Sita that mother, father, brother help to some extent only but the husband helps in getting the salvation and the wife who disregards her husband is unreligious.

When they were passing through the forest, Viradha, a demon attacked them. Both Rama and Lakshman thrashed him to death as weapons could not kill him. After killing him, all the three reached the hermitage of sage Agastya and touched his feet. Sage Agastya told Rama that he (Rama) is like God to all saints and sages and his mission is to free the earth from the burden of demons. Sage Agastya advised Rama to live in Panchavati. On their way to Panchavati, they met Jatayu – a vulture who promised that he would protect Sita. They reached Panchavati, Rama was very happy to see its scenic beauty. He asked Lakshman to choose a good site and make a hut. Lakshman obeyed his brother and they started living there. All the sages and saints became free from the terrors of demons.

One day Shorpanakha, the sister of Ravana came and talked to Rama with a smiling face that, "there is no man like you and no woman like me in the three universes. I have fallen in love with you and want you to be my husband." On this Rama told her that he is already married and she could propose to his younger brother Lakshmana. Then Shorpanakha went to Lakshmana and proposed marriage to him which he refused and struck off her nose and both the ears. She was crying and looking horrible and went to her brothers Khara, Dushana and Trisara. Shorpanakha's brothers could not bear the insult of their sister, they started marching with their army of demon soldiers. Rama asked Lakshmana to take Sita to a mountain cave for her safety. Rama was fighting alone and killed Khara, Dushana and Trisara. Thereafter, Shorpanakha went to her brother Ravana and explained the whole story. Ravana went to Mareecha for help and explained to him his plan to kidnap Sita. He advised Mareecha to turn himself into a golden deer and roam in front of Rama's hut. When Sita saw the golden deer, she got attracted and requested Rama for its skin. Rama told Lakshman to look after Sita in his absence and ran after the deer with bow and arrows. Mareecha took Rama far away from his hut, so that Ravana could get time to kidnap Sita. Finally, Rama shot an arrow which pierced the deer's body. He started imitating Rama's voice and cried out the name of Lakshmana for help. On hearing the voice, Sita requested Lakshmana to go out and

Lakshmana struck off nose and both ears of Shurparakha

help his brother. Since Lakshmana knew that no one in the world could kill Rama, he kept on denying to go. Sita then used some unpleasant words to

Sita seeing the golden deer

Lakshmana which led him to go but before going, he drew a holy demarcation line around the hut and told Sita not to cross the line. As soon as Lakshmana left, Ravana who was hiding there transformed himself into a sage and asked Sita for food. She brought the food but did not cross the demarcation line which Ravana insisted. As Ravana was going back without taking food, Sita came out of the line. He caught hold of her and put her in his chariot. Sita screamed

Sita kidnapped by Ravana

and called for help to Rama and Lakshmana. Suddenly, Jatayu who was sitting on a tree saw Sita with Ravana, he came to rescue Sita but Ravana cut off his wings, he fell down on the earth and Ravana flew away with Sita. He kept Sita in Ashok Vatika. When Rama and Lakshmana reached the cottage, they found it deserted, and started searching for Sita here and there but in vain. They saw Jatayu lying in a pool of blood, he was wounded and groaning in pain. He told Rama before his death that Ravana had kidnapped Sita, he tried to save Sita and fought with Ravana but Ravana cut off his wings with his sword, he had gone towards the south with Sita. Rama and Lakshmana performed the last rites of Jatayu. They went in the direction which Jatayu told them. On the way they met Kabandh, a Gandharva who informed them about Sabri. As they reached the hermitage of Sabri, who was waiting eagerly for Rama, her joy knew no bounds and she fed them with sweet beri fruits. After being told about the kidnapping of Sita by Ravana, Sabri advised Rama to meet Sugreeva at the Rishyamooka mountain who would help Rama to find Sita. Lord Rama and Lakshmana thanked Sabri and moved ahead.

Rama meeting with Shabari

Importance: Tulsidas says that those people are great who leave everything except Shri Hari/Lord Rama.

Kishkindha Kaand

(This episode relates to the march of Lord Rama and Lakshmana towards Rishyamooka mountain, meeting with

Hanuman and Sugreeva, death of Bali, coronation of Sugreeva as the king of Kishkindha and the search for Sita by monkeys and bears in the army of Sugreeva.)

Rama meeting Hanuman

Lord Rama and Lakshmana reached Rishyamooka mountain as told by Sabri where Sugreeva, the king of Vanars was living. When Sugreeva saw both Rama and Lakshmana coming towards him, he had the suspicion that his elder brother Bali might have sent them to kill him. He, therefore, sent Hanuman disguised as a Brahmin in order to know the truth about them. Hanumanji went to Rama and Lakshmana

Death of Bali by Rama

and asked them who they were and why they were roaming

in this dense forest. Rama replied that they were the sons of Dashratha, the king of Ayodhya and their names were Rama and Lakshmana. Sita, wife of Rama was kidnapped by Ravana, therefore they were moving in the forests in search of her. They were also looking for Sugreeva who would help them in their search for Sita.

Hanumanji recognised Lord Rama and fell at his feet. Hanuman carried both Rama and Lakshmana on his shoulders through airway and reached the abode of Sugreeva, he introduced both of them to Sugreeva who assured Rama that his army would trace out Sita. Then Sugreeva told Rama about his woeful story of his elder brother Bali who had great love and affection for him but due to a misunderstanding, he wanted to kill him, Bali also deprived him of his wife. Rama assured Sugreeva not to worry as his wife and kingdom would be regained. Then Sugreeva showed Rama and Lakshmana some ornaments thrown by Sita from the sky, looking at them, Rama became emotional.

In a duel between Sugreeva and Bali, Lord Rama shot an arrow which pierced through Bali's chest and he died. Sugreeva became the king of Kishkindha and Angada the son of Bali became the prince. After becoming the king, Sugreeva started living a luxurious life in his palace and forgot about the promise which he had given to Rama. Then Rama sent Lakshmana to make Sugreeva aware of his duty. Sugreeva felt very ashamed of his deeds and gave orders to his army with four groups to find out Sitaji in the four directions. Sugreeva sent Hanuman, Angad, Jambavan, Nal, Nil, etc. in the south. Rama gave his ring to Hanuman to give the same to Sita for consoling her.

Rama giving his ring to Hanuman

Hanuman with his group went very far in search of Sita. They were tired, hungry and thirsty. Suddenly, their eyes fell on a cave from where birds were flying out full of joy. When they entered the cave, they saw trees laden with fruits. The whole area was guarded by a woman yogi – but when she came to know that they were to serve Lord Rama, she gave them permission to refresh themselves. She transported all of them to the seashore by virtue of her yoga *shakti*. There they met Sampati, the brother of Jatayu who informed Hanuman that Ravana had kept Sita in Ashok Vatika in Lanka. All the members of the group became very delighted to know the whereabouts of Sita and started discussing it. Jambhavan inspired Hanuman to cross the sea and achieve the goal. He even reminded Hanuman about the story when he was a child. Once he looked at the sun and thought it was a fruit, he flew towards the sun to eat it. At this Indra attacked him with his *Vajra* in order to protect the sun from his clutches. Indra's *Vajra* broke Hanuman's right jaw and he fell down on a mountain.

Seeing this, Hanuman's father Wind God got annoyed and he stopped his movements. With the result, all living beings felt suffocated because of no air. Then all the gods apologised to Wind and blessed Hanumna. Brahma and Indra showered boons that no weapon can slay him and death could not come to him without Hanuman's will.

Importance: Lord Rama who is beautiful like Kamdeva, one must hear of his character with devotion.

Sundar Kaand

(The episode relates to finding out the whereabouts of Sitaji, going of Hanuman to Ashok Vatika and its destruction by him, dragging of Hanuman to the court of Ravana in Lanka, wrapping of Hanuman's tail with rags dipped in oil and set on fire, burning of Lanka and finally the return of Hanuman and his description of Lanka and the details of finding Sita to Lord Rama.)

After visiting Jambavan, Hanuman realised his strength and courage and leaped towards Lanka. The gods sent Surasa, mother of serpents to test the wisdom, intelligence and strength of Hanuman. Hanuman succeeded, therefore, Surasa blessed him and told Hanuman that he would surely fulfil the mission of Lord Rama and then she disappeared into the sea. Hanuman then flew towards Lanka. On the way, he met another demon named Simhika, who used to catch creatures flying in the sky by just capturing their shadow. She caught hold of Hanuman and swallowed him but Hanuman tore open her body and ripped a way out through her stomach.

At last he reached Lanka and climbed up a high hill in order to have a look at entire Lanka. Hanuman saw the beauty of Lanka which was guarded by Lankini. He decided to enter

Lanka in the darkness of the night, therefore, reduced his body stature, so that nobody could see him. There he met Vibhishana who explained everything about Sita to him. Thereupon Hanuman went to the Ashok Vatika where he heard Ravana was talking to Sita that he would make her his queen and all other queens would be ruled by her. On hearing this, Hanuman got angry but he controlled himself; when Ravana went back, all the demonesses starting frightening Sita but one of them Trijata stopped them from doing so. After their departure, Hanuman jumped down from the tree and stood before Sita with folded hands giving her Lord Rama's ring and telling her that he was a messenger of Lord Rama. Rama and Lakshmana would come to Lanka and take her away, therefore, she should not worry anymore. Since Hanuman was feeling hungry, he took permission from Sita to eat fruits from Ashok Vatika. He uprooted many trees and threw the fruits on the ground, thus destroying Ashok Vatika. When the guards came to know this, they came there to kill Hanuman but they were all thrashed by him. When Ravana came to know this, he sent his son Aksha Kumar with an army, Hanuman killed Aksha and his army. Then Ravana sent his son Meghnada known as Indrajit to capture Hanuman. Meghnada shot *Brahmastra* towards Hanuman and Hanuman allowed himself to be bound with the *Brahmastra*. Hanuman was thus dragged to the court of Ravana, where he introduced himself as a messenger of Lord Rama.

Ravana ordered his men to wrap Hanuman's tail with rags dipped in oil and set on fire. Hanuman resumed his large size and jumped from house to house and thus Lanka was soon burning in flames. The whole Lanka was burnt except Ashok Vatika and the house of Vibhishana. Then he plunged into the sea to put off the fire of his tail. After that

Hanuman burning Lanka with his tail which was dipped in oil and set on fire in the court of Ravana

he went to Sita and bowed before her. Sita gave him *churamani* as a proof that he had met Sita. Hanuman returned back across the sea. All the members of his group who were waiting for him felt very happy and started jumping with joy. Then all of them proceeded towards Kishkindha to convey the message of Sita to Lord Rama and Sugreeva. Hanuman met Lord Rama and informed him about Sita and gave him the *churamani/ shikhamani* given by Sita. On seeing the *churamani*, Rama started crying, remembering the sweet moments spent with her.

Rama embraces Hanumana after conveying the message of Sita

Lord Rama called Sugreeva to get ready. All reached near the seashore but the main problem before them was of crossing the vast sea. Rama prayed to the Sea-God for three days but it did not bring any effect. On this Rama got angry and decided to dry the sea with his arrows. As he took out an arrow out of his quiver, the Sea-God appeared on the water with folded hands and told Rama about the two monkeys Nala and Neela of his army who had the boon that anything touched by them would float on water.

On the other hand, Ravana called a meeting of his ministers and commanders to chalk out the next course of action. Vibhishana, Ravana's brother told Ravana that he had not done good by kidnapping Sita, thus brought trouble on the head of the demon's race. On this, Ravana got angry and gave a blow to Vibhishana with his leg. When Vibhishana saw that Ravana is determined in his decision, he thought of seeking place in the feet of Lord Rama. He, therefore, crossed the sea and reached where Rama camped with his army. Rama embraced him and crowned him with sea water.

Importance: The chanting of Rama's qualities leads to good omens. Those who listen to it without any doubt will get salvation.

Lanka Kaand

(The episode relates to the building of a bridge on the sea with the help of Nala and Neela, its crossing by Lord Rama and his army, sending of Angad as a peace messenger in the court of Ravana and the denial of Ravana, attack on Lanka, and the end of Kumbhakaran, Meghnada and Ravana, coronation of Vibhishana, meeting of Lord Rama with Sita, boarding of the *Pushpaka Vimana* by Lord Rama, Lakshmana, Sita, Hanuman and others towards Ayodhya.)

A bridge was built on the sea with the help of Nala and Neela and other monkeys. As Nala and Neela had the boon that anything touched by them would float on water, monkeys brought huge trees and pieces of stones from the forest, Nala and Neela touched them and wrote Sri Rama on them, threw them in the sea and they floated. Thus, the bridge was built.

Building of a bridge on the sea

After seeing the bridge, Lord Rama called the sages and a Shiva Linga was established. After performing the *puja*, Lord Rama informed that no one is as lovable as Shiva and those who are against Shiva are not lovable to me even in dreams.

Brahma's and other Devtas blessing to Rama after building of the bridge on the sea

Lord Rama crossed the sea along with the others and camped on the shore of Lanka. Ravana's wife Mandodri advised Ravana not to oppose Lord Rama as his birth was for relieving the earth from the atrocities of demons. She advised him to hand over

Sita to Lord Rama and after coronation of his son Meghnath to recide in the jungles and recite the name of Lord Rama. But Ravana did not pay any heed to her.

Rama worshipping the Shiva Lina before Crossing the sea

Before starting the war, one more effort was made to persuade Ravana, Angad was sent in the court of Ravana as a peace messenger requesting Ravana to return back Sita to Lord Rama but Ravana was firm in his decision. Angad challenged Ravana and othes if anybody could shake his feet from the ground, he would go back without Sita but nobody was able to lift his feet. At last, Ravana got up and touched the feet of Angad in order to lift him but Angad told him instead of touching his feet, why did he not touch the feet of Lord Rama. After hearing this, Ravana returned to his seat and Angad came back and explained all to Lord Rama. Seeing no hope of peace from anywhere, finally war was declared.

The first battle took place between Meghnath and Hanuman who gave a blow with his leg on Meghnath's chest. On seeing this, his charioteer took him away from the battlefield. The second battle which took place between Meghnadth was with Lakshmana who smashed his chariot in anger. Seeing this, Meghnadth shot the Brahmastra and Lakshmana fell into a swoon. Rama put Lakshmana's head on his lap and started crying. Hanuman went to Lanka to bring Sushena, an Ayurveda acharya who had a cure for the *Brahmastra*. Sushena told the name of the medicine

Lakshmana's head in Rama's lap after Meghnanda shot Brahm Astra

and mountain from where the herb had to be procured. After seeking blessings of Rama, Hanuman flew towards the Himalayas. On reaching the peak, he got confused while identifying the herb and with no option left, he uprooted the whole Kailash mountain and flew back.

Hanuman after getting confused to identity the medicine/herb uprooted the Kailash and bringing it

On the way, he met Kalnemi demon sent by Ravana but Hanuman killed him. When Hanuman reached near Nandigram, Bharat mistaking him for a demon, shot an arrow at Hanuman. With the result, he fell on the ground with the word 'Rama'. Bharat immediately rushed to the spot where Hanuman was lying unconscious and revived him. Then Hanuman told Bharat the whole story. Bharat fell sad and ashamed of himself as without thinking he struck down Hanuman. He requested Hanuman to save his brother Lakshmana. He told Hanuman that he would host an arrow, Hanuman could sit on that and reach Lanka in time. Hanuman thanked Bharat and reached Lanka. Everybody became very happy to see Hanuman. Sushena took off some of the leaves of *Mritsanjivana* and dropped its juice in Lakshman's mouth and applied the paste on his chest. After a few minutes, Lakshmana got up.

On the other hand, Ravana ordered his servants to make efforts to wake his younger brother Kumbhkarana who was very huge in size and had the boon from Lord Brahma to remain asleep for six months in a year. It was very difficult to arouse him. With great difficulty, he got up and went to Ravana who explained to him the entire story. He advised Ravana to go back to Rama's fold but Ravana did not listen to him. He walked into the battlefield but was killed by Lord Rama and attained salvation.

After regaining consciousness, Lakshmana got up and asked about Meghnath and was told that he is performing a *yajna* which would make him invincible. Lakshmana along with Hanuman, Vibhishana and others went to the place where Meghanth was performing the *yajna*. A battle took place between Meghnath and Lakshmana wherein Meghnada was killed. When he was dying, he called the names of Rama and Lakshmana. Hanuman took the body of Meghnath and put it before the main entrance of Lanka and returned back.

When Ravana heard about the death of his son Meghnath, he became very upset and fell down unconscious on the earth.

His wife Mandodri also cried when she saw the body of her son Meghnath. Then many battles took place between Ravana and Rama and Lakshmana. In anger, Ravana shot *Brahmastra* which went to Lakshmana chest due to which he fell down but after listening to the words of Lord Rama, Lakshmana got up. Then Ravana shot the *Prachanda Shakti*. Lord Rama saved Vibhishana and he took the shot on himself. At last, Vibhishana advised Lord Rama to target the navel portion of Ravana which contained nectars and kept him alive.

So Rama targeted towards the navel of Ravana and shot a divine arrow due to which the nectar in his navel got dried up. He fell down on the ground with the word 'Rama'. Hearing of the death of Ravana, gods in the heaven showered flowers on him. They were feeling very happy as the cause of their fear was no more. Seeing Ravana's body, Vibhishana cried but Lord Rama consoled him by saying that Ravana

Rama fighting with Ravana

fought like a hero, death had washed all his sins and he had gone to heaven. He advised Vibhishana to perform the last rites of Ravana. After that, Lord Rama sent Lakshmana with Hanuman, Sugreeva, Angada, Jambavan and others to Lanka for the coronation ceremony of Vibhishana. He was seated on the throne of Lanka and Lakshmana applied the *tilak* on his forehead and crowned him the king of Lanka. Lord Rama, Sita, Lakshmana, Hanuman, Nala, Neela and others boarded the *Pushpaka Viman* and proceeded towards Ayodhya. Rama showed all the places to Sita where they had stayed and taken rest.

Importance: Tulsidas says that those who hear of Lord Rama, God gives them victory, mind and fame. There is no other way in this *Kalyug* except to remember the name of Rama.

Uttra Kaand

(This episode relates to the warm welcome by the people of Ayodhya when Lord Rama, Sita, Lakshmana, Hanuman and others reached there, coronation of Lord Rama and the establishment *Rama Rajya*.)

Coronation of Rama in Ayodhya

Lord Rama reached Ayodhya along with Sita, Lakshmana and his army. Guru Vashista, Bharat, Shatrugan, three mothers Kaushalya, Kaikeyee and Sumitra met them. Lord Rama called Sugreeva, Nala, Neela, Angad, Hanuman and

Rama, Lakshman, Sita and Hanuman reached Ayodhya

Jamvan and introduced them by saying that they helped him a lot in the war with Ravana, even did not hesitate to sacrifice their own lives, they were dearer to him than Bharat. Sage Vashishtha called the brahmins for the coronation ceremony of Lord Rama. Sumantra collected all the pious things needed for the ceremony and Ayodhya was decorated like a new bride. Lord Rama called Bharat, combed his hair and told all the three brothers to take bath. After that, Lord Rama opened his own hair and took a bath. After taking a bath, he wore clothes and jewels. Sita was also dressed in new clothes and jewellery by her mothers-in-law and was sitting on the left side of Lord Rama. First of all, sage Vashishtha put tilak on the forehead of Lord Rama, then followed the other brahmins.

In this way six months passed. Lord Rama called for new clothes and beautiful jewellery for Sugreeva, Nala, Neela, Angad, Jamvan, Nishad Raj and advised them to return back to their respective places and to lead their lives as per their minds, *karma* and the rights. The people of Ayodhya were feeling very happy after Lord Rama became their king. People loved each other, they were leading life as per the teachings of the Vedas. All the three brothers had a great regard for their elder brother Lord Rama, who also used to teach them the good things. Sita gave birth to two sons – Lava and Kusha. The other brothers also had two sons each. Sitaji used to serve her mothers-in-law with due respect, there was no ego amongst them. There was no enemy in *Rama Rajya*. Nobody used to commit any crime, therefore, no verdict was given.

Rama Rajya

Once Lord Rama spoke – one gets this human body with great difficulty the body leads to *Sadhana* and *Nirvana/ Moksha*. One who has not attended *moksha* repents in the end and suffers. After getting the body, one should not indulge oneself in worldly things, such people drink poison instead of *Amrita*. The body is like a ship which has to cross the *Bhav sagar* and *Satguru* is the one who constructs this ship. If one wants to get happiness in this world or beyond it, then listen to my words and keep it in your heart with determination. To obtain *Gyan*/knowledge is a difficult path and there are many hurdles while attaining it. *Bhakti* is independent and gives happiness but one cannot get it without *Satsang*. After folding his hands, Lord Rama said that without worshipping Shiva, one cannot attain my *Bhakti*. One who follows the *Bhakti marg* need not do any *yagna, japa, tapa* or fast. One should have a good nature/character, and feel satisfaction/ happiness in whatever one gets. One should not quarrel with others, do not expect from anyone and also not to fear.

Ramacharita Manas is pious and when human values are degenerating and one finds oneself in darkness, it acts as a guiding light. The ideals of love, tolerance, sacrifice and other virtues which it teaches us would help us to tackle the difficulties of life.

Importance: All the characters of the Ramcharita Manas perform their duties very well. Kaushalya the mother of Lord Rama is shown as an ideal mother who forgets the deeds of Kaikeyee and treats Bharat like her own son Rama. Lord Rama is an ideal son. He considered the orders of his father Dashratha beyond anything else, that is why he is being called '*Maryada Purushottam*'. Ramacharitra Manas also defines the love of one brother for another. Where Lakshmana went along with Lord Rama to the jungle, on the other hand, Bharat did not accept himself as the king of Ayodhya and put Lord Rama's wooden slippers on the throne.

Hanumanji is an example of a real devotee, who is always ready in the service of Lord Rama. Anger/egoism is the root cause of destruction and the same is seen in the character of Ravana. A person can take lessons/inspiration from the characters of Ramacharitra Manas and adopt them in their lives. Those who read, listen and sing about the character of Lord Rama, they get *Moksha*/Salvation easily. If one recites, understands even four or five verses of Ramacharitra Manas and keep them in their hearts, Lord Rama takes away all their miseries/sorrows.

❑❑❑